THE 1ST AMERICAN COOKIE LADY

RECIPES FROM
A 1917 COOKIE DIARY

BY
BARBARA SWELL

mama

anna "Cookie" Covington

"This makes 208 different kinds of cookies."
~Anna "Cookie" Covington

ISBN 978-1-883206-49-9   Order No. NGB-839
Library of Congress Control Number: 2005926786
©2005 by Native Ground Music, Inc.
Asheville, North Carolina

THE LOST COOKIE JOURNAL

The FIRST American cookie lady? No kidding. I found her. Not only did I find cookie lady Anna "Cookie" Covington, I believe her long-lost cookie journal was America's first cookie cookbook! Let me introduce you to Mrs. Covington and tell you how I came to discover her cookie diary.

I landed Anna's 76-page handwritten cookie cookbook at an Ebay auction in October of 2004. One look at the description and photos of this unassuming journal had me hooting and hollering, as I knew this was the earliest written collection of cookie recipes in America that I had ever seen. Hoping against hope that I'd end up with what promised to be an extraordinary treasure, I lucked out and won the bid against some fierce competition. Unfortunately, I wasn't able to find out where the journal was purchased other than somewhere in the Pacific Northwest. However, it's been fun to piece together little clues Anna left in her cookbook to get a hint of what her daily life was like.

Not unlike this special recipe diary, all vintage handwritten cooking journals are a portal into the kitchens of the past. Read between the lines, and there you are...smack-dab in the middle of the heart of the home where Mother's baking sugar cookies in the cook stove while mixing up a diphtheria remedy at the sink for fear that the deadly disease might come calling for her young'uns.

Anna's journal tells the story of a loving mother who was flat eat up with cookie-baking, determined to pass her passion on to at least one of her kids. Reading the recipes, we know that she was not a farmer. Many of her sources were popular women's magazines such as *The Modern Priscilla* and *Ladies Home Journal* and not family farming magazines like *Farm Journal and Farmer's Wife* or *Successful Farming.* I'm guessing she lived in a small town, not a large city.

Fortunately, Anna dated many of her recipes, so we know that they were recorded during the years between 1917 and 1920. As it happens, these were the same years in which Americans were asked to conserve food in order to feed our troops and allies during World War I. We get a glimpse of how the war touched Anna's life as she volunteered to do her patriotic duty to do with less of every ingredient it takes to make a decent cookie.

THE LOST COOKIE JOURNAL

So how is it that this passionate cookie lady left a beautifully penned cookie diary that was never used? You heard me right; there's not a smidgen of splattered batter in the book. The lovely, hand-scripted pages were barely leafed through. Did Anna's husband die fighting in the war and that's why she had no daughter to pass her cookbook to? Was she unable to bear children, or did her daughter die during the flu pandemic of 1918? Maybe she had sons and none of them baked. How did the book slip out of the family? Unless, by some good fortune, her descendants recognize her from this cookbook, the mystery will remain unsolved.

Just in case you're wondering if Anna was really America's first cookie lady and this book of hers was the first American cookie cookbook, let me chat with you a minute about why I think this is so.

While there had been American confectionery cookbooks printed in the 19th century, there were, to my knowledge, no cookie cookbooks published prior to the 1920's, probably with good reason. One look at Anna's collection of recipes and you'll notice that half of them aren't very good. Fascinating, but they're not like the cookies that we know and love today. While cookies of European descent were quite tasty, American cookies in Anna's day were more like little cakes. Bland and puffy. In fact, cakes were the "in" dessert in the 19th and early 20th centuries, and I'll bet there were plenty of "cake ladies" back then. Cookies tagged along after the cake recipes in period cookbooks, and wouldn't even get their own chapter until around 1910, let alone a whole cookbook.

If early cookies didn't taste that great, why did Anna go to the trouble to collect 208 different recipes for them? When you look at the sugar cookies and molasses/ginger cookies, you'll notice very little difference between the many recipes. She collected just about ALL of the cookie recipes that were popular during the years between 1917 and 1920. Only a cookie lady with a vision would do such a thing. She saw endless possibilities for putting a creative thumbprint on this quaint dessert that would take off like gangbusters by the 1930's.

Thank goodness Anna thought to put her passion for cookies in writing. By a curious twist of fate, YOU get to be the first one to bake cookies out of Anna's long-lost cookie journal. I think she'd be happy to see some spice cookie batter smeared about the pages, so dig in and bake up some fun!

ABOUT THE RECIPES

E ven the most ragged antique cooking journal deserves great respect. One little alteration is all it takes and you've defiled the manuscript and changed history. And so I had great misgivings about changing the order of Anna's recipes. It felt like breaking up a family and creating a bunch of little recipe orphans. There's so much to be told by just reading the order of Anna's cookies, like who and where she visited, her exotic flavoring extract phase, the arrival of her newest *Modern Priscilla* magazine, and the effects of ingredient shortages brought on by World War I.

Knowing full-well the risks, I made the executive decision that Anna wouldn't give a lump of cookie dough for her lovingly recorded journal to be read for historic interest and then retired to the living room bookshelf, perhaps forever. No, she would have been thrilled to imagine a space-age mom offering her grinning kids a plate of Auntie Anna's Fairy Cookies cut into fancy shapes and sprinkled with colored sugar. Today's everyday cookie baker probably isn't going to sift through 208 handwritten old-timey recipes in hodge-podge order to find just the right gingersnap. Here's how this user-friendly version is set up:

Each of Anna's recipes is numbered in the order in which she recorded them. The numbered recipes are untouched, spelling errors and all.

Though Anna's cookies may have been modern at the time, some of her recipes don't taste so great by today's standards. Below many of them you will find alternate recipes that are more suitable to current preferences...or should I say more suitable to our tasters' preferences! Fortunately, we had a never-ending supply of volunteer taste-testers ranging in age from 4 to 90. Some of the alternate recipes are from post-1920 vintage cookbooks, and some are my suggestions based on taster recommendations.

While Anna recorded her material from about 1917 through 1920, many of her recipes are from a much earlier era, and I've attempted to document the origin of some of them, where possible. Graphics and photographs range in age from the mid-19th century up through the 1940's.

For a copy of Anna's actual manuscript, contact Native Ground Music at the address on the last page of the book.

TABLE OF CONTENTS

Each of Anna's recipes is numbered in the order in which she recorded them. The numbered recipes are untouched, spelling errors and all.

Kids & The Cookie Jar

THE COOKY TREE

My mother asked my father
  To plant a cooky tree—
She needed one at once, she said,
  To grow a crop for me.

My father said, "I'll plant one,
  If you'll select the kind,
For quite a large variety
  Of cooky trees you'll find."

My mother said she'd ask me
  The kind I'd like to grow—
But which I truly like the best,
  I really do not know.

If I should plant just "macaroons,"
  Then "brownies" wouldn't be—
I guess I'll need an orchard
  Instead of just one tree!

~*Tummy Tingles,* Wheat Flour Institute, 1937

Kids & The Cookie Jar

Pre-1900 cookies were typically high in flour and low in sweetness. Anna's old-fashioned sugar and molasses cookies were still evolving from cakes and you'll likely find that they have too much flour, and not enough butter or sugar for today's adult tastes. Assuming that kids would scoff at these cakey cookies, I was surprised to find that they were well-received by the 8-to-10 year old crowd when I brought them in for several classroom cookie tastings this year. Children prefer uncomplicated flavors, especially if they don't find anything mysterious like raisins or nuts in their mouths.

You'll feel much better about offering your kids one of these cookies instead of a head-sized, calorie-laden, gooey, chocolaty, greasy, mall-bought cookie. So feel free to keep the cookie jar full of Anna's modest-sized, wholesome, old-fashioned cookies.

Photo courtesy Library of Congress

A house should have a cookie jar for when it's half past three,
And children hurry home from school as hungry as can be,
There's nothing quite so splendid in filling children up,
As spicy, fluffy ginger cakes and sweet milk in a cup.
A house should have a mother waiting with a hug,
No matter what a boy brings home-a puppy or a bug.
For children only loiter when the bell rings to dismiss,
If no one's home to greet them with a cookie and a kiss.

~ Author Unknown

COOKIE-BAKING TIPS

To whiney, perfectionist, or beginning bakers: If you need specific directions for baking, you will find this book full of vague directions exceedingly annoying. If you're new to cookie baking, there are many great baking books that can instruct you on technique.

To the rest of you who enjoy history and are adventurous, throw-things-together type cooks, get ready for some fun.

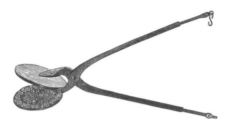

A Few Tips

- Preheat your oven.
- Make half a recipe so you can see if you like the cookie.
- Always bake a test cookie, then adjust ingredients according to taste.
- Add a pinch of salt to most recipes if you're using unsalted butter.
- Use unsalted butter! (makes for a much better cookie)
- Flours take a few minutes to absorb the moisture from your dough, so after you mix your batter, wait a few minutes before adding more flour than the recipe suggests.
- Bake cookies on parchment paper.
- If baking more than one sheet of cookies at a time, quickly switch sheets and reverse them when half-baked.
- Cool cookies on a wire rack, then store in an airtight container.

Rules for Cookie Baking, 1924

1. Wash your hands with soap and water.
2. Have your hair neatly fastened back.
3. Wear no jewelry.
4. Wear a wash dress.
5. Clean up your work.
6. Hang a piece of paper on the oven door when the oven is in use to remind you of the baking.

28. DROP COOKIES

For drop cookie receipt out of cake batter, always allow about 1 cup extra of flour to any cake recipe to make the batter about right to obtain shape.

A quick oven is a necissity, as this forms the cookie before it has a chance to spread itself very much. Flour differs greatly, of course, but about 5 cups are needed with a recipe that calls for a cup each of butter & milk & 3 or 4 eggs. However, a sample takes but a minute & may save the 1st pan of cookies.

When baking cookies, if you burn a panful, it is a sign of news from distant friends.   ~Sloan's Cookbook, 1901

Water cookies keep longer than milk cookies.   ~The Cook Not Mad, 1831

Photo courtesy Library of Congress

EQUIPMENT

To make all of the cookies in this book, you'll need:

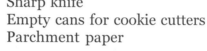

A mixing bowl
Mixer or beaters
Cup   Spatula
Spoon
Cookie sheet
Sharp knife
Empty cans for cookie cutters
Parchment paper

Sifter

As you can see, I'm the last person on earth who should be telling you what equipment you need in order to bake cookies. I don't have anything fancier or more modern in my kitchen than Anna had in hers 100 years ago. Except for my $15 portable mixer and refrigerator. It's not that I have anything against kitchen gadgets, I just don't want anything else junking up my life, and I've been cooking so long I can eyeball ingredients fairly accurately. The only thing I really urge you to purchase is parchment paper. It will make your cookies turn out great. You can reuse each sheet about five times.

Cookie Cutters

With at least half of Anna's's recipes calling for the dough to be rolled and cut, we're left to ponder, "cut with what?" The only clues we have are to "cut jumbles in rounds and cut out the center with a thimble," and for forming fig bars, "a mustard-box with hole punched in the bottom makes a good cutter." Though fancy 19th century cookie cutters are much sought after by today's collectors, I don't think you would have found them in Anna's cupboard. I'm guessing her circle cutter looked a lot like this empty can of baking powder!

Rolling cookie cutter

EQUIPMENT

Anna took several of her recipes from *The Modern Priscilla*, a popular woman's handwork and homemaking magazine in the 1910's.

MEASUREMENT

All measurements are inexact. If "flour enough to make a soft dough" is good enough for Anna, by golly, it's good enough for me. Besides, I don't have anything to measure with, myself, except a glass pyrex cup whose red numbers have long worn off. Unfortunately for you, I did most of the recipe testing.

You know, it wasn't until the 1880's that cooks started carefully measuring their ingredients. We have Fannie Merritt Farmer and her ilk to thank, or I would say curse, for that. Known as "the mother of modern measurement," she was part of the domestic science movement in the late 1800's that transformed housewifery and cooking from what some viewed as a prison sentence to an exact and respectable science. If you ask me, the whole cooking school movement was the beginning of the end of good cooking in America.

Early to mid-19th century cookbooks are just full of minimally measured, wholesome foods made from fresh dairy products, lightly cooked, thoughtfully spiced garden vegetables, and breads made from a variety of grains. Some of the old meat dishes make me a bit queasy, but that might just be because I'm not used to eating pickled tongue and tripe.

All you have to do is look at the Boston Cooking-School of Culinary Science and Domestic Economics magazine (*American Cookery*) to see what sort of things the modern housewife was thinking she had to prepare for her family in 1920. Can't you just imagine the fallen faces of father and children as mother presents the new obscenely tall foods with things like asparagus and celery artfully poking out every which-way? Oh, and what queasy price was paid by the serving of wiggly seasick gelatin dishes with grapes and radishes suspended forever in Jell-O purgatory?

Surely Anna didn't succumb to the lure of carefully measured, dainty, shaky desserts, not with a nickname like "Cookie." With one foot in the 19th century and the other in the kitchen of the modern 20th century housewife, she was a woman who jumped on the cookie cart before it came to town. I doubt Anna, herself, ever measured much of anything.

MEASUREMENT

T he only measurements in this book that might pose a problem for American cooks will be those written in weights. Unlike recipes from culinary experts of today that require measurements in weight for accuracy, these recipes are holdovers from their European ancestors. Isn't that wonderful? We have no way of knowing how much the ingredients in Anna's day actually weighed, for sugars and flours were different then. However, since this is a book of "make-do" cooking, here are some very general guidelines:

1 cup sugar = 8 oz.
1 teacup sugar = supposedly 8 oz., but I only measure 6 oz.
1 cup milk or cream = about 8 oz.
1 cup butter = 2 sticks = 8 oz.
3-4 cups flour = 1 lb. (Most vintage cookbooks state that there are four cups of flour to a pound. All the white, unbleached flours I've used weigh about 6 oz. per cup, unsifted.)

To Mix Dough:
About half of Anna's recipes direct the baker to mix "stiff" or "soft." Aren't we lucky to have such flexibility!

Mix Soft is typically a dough containing cream or other liquids which will produce a soft cookie. Any cookie that is to be rolled out will need to be refrigerated first so that it's easier to handle. Otherwise, you'll keep adding flour and bake up crackers instead of cookies. Soft mixed cookies are not easy to roll out, so I just usually form the dough into logs and roll them up in waxed paper, freeze, then slice and bake.

Mix Stiff means add more flour than "mix soft." Maybe a wooden spoon will stand up in the batter, or you can roll the dough unchilled, or you can use it to chink your log cabin. You'll figure it out!

MEASUREMENT

You can see what earlier generations of cooks were up against when you look at this measurement conversion chart from *The White House Cook Book*, 1887.

IN ORDINARY USE AMONG HOUSEKEEPERS

4 Teaspoonfuls equal 1 tablespoonful liquid.

4 Tablespoonfuls equal 1 wine-glass, or half a gill.

2 Wine-glasses equal one gill or half a cup.

2 Gills equal 1 coffeecupful, or 16 tablespoonfuls.

2 Coffeecupfuls equal 1 pint.

To measure a teaspoon

2 Pints equal 1 quart.

4 Quarts equal 1 gallon.

2 Tablespoonfuls equal 1 ounce, liquid.

1 Tablespoonful of salt equals 1 ounce.

Half a teaspoon

16 Ounces equal 1 pound, or a pint of liquid.

4 Coffeecupfuls of sifted flour equal 1 pound.

1 Quart of unsifted flour equals 1 pound.

8 or 10 ordinary sized eggs equal 1 pound.

1 Pint of sugar equals 1 pound. (White granulated.)

A quarter teaspoon

2 Coffeecupfuls of powdered sugar equal 1 pound.

1 Coffeecupful of cold butter, pressed down, is one-half pound.

1 Tablespoonful of soft butter, well rounded, equals 1 ounce.

An ordinary tumblerful equals 1 coffeecupful, or half a pint.

About 25 drops of any thin liquid will fill a common sized teaspoon.

Photo courtesy Library of Congress

INGREDIENTS

Flu pandemic and World War I aside, the years between 1917 and 1920 were better in some ways than today, nearly a century hence. Of course, if I lay dying of an infection for want of antibiotics, I might think otherwise. So, let's just stick to discussing baking ingredients. Butter, sugar, flour, and eggs. Until recent years, the modern American cookie baker who headed to the local grocery for supplies, ended up with a shopping cart full of margarine, refined sugar, bleached flour, and watery pale eggs.

It was a sad occasion, indeed, at my own house when, in 1969, my family's supply of home-delivered farm-fresh eggs abruptly ended. Turns out my mother got miffed at the egg man for walking in unannounced one day, as usual, with his weekly carton of eggs. Only this time, he caught her in her skivvies as she readied herself for the day. That was the end of the egg man, and that was the end of the dark-yolked farm eggs. Until I left home and discovered chickens. Annoying and stinky as they are to raise, you gotta love the eggs. Nowadays, 21st-century bakers don't have to settle for insipid grocery store eggs. Most of us can patronize our local food co-op and summer tailgate markets, as well as year-round farmer's markets and pick up locally farmed eggs. The same goes for butter, only you'll pay dearly for it.

"Always use the best materials," says the author of *Quick Cooking* in 1885. "Fresh eggs, pure milk, sweet butter and lard, the best brands of baking powder, the purest spices and extracts, will insure unvarying success. Inferior materials destroy the chemical conditions under which various ingredients unite, and lead to frequent and mortifying failures." So do as you're told, dear. You don't want to bake mortifying cookies, now do you?

INGREDIENTS

When she could get them, Anna would have baked with farm eggs, salted butter, and pure, packaged white flour. (Up until the Pure Food and Drug act of 1906, store-bought flour was often laced with adulterants like chalk in order to stretch it.) She might have ordered her baking powders, spices and flavoring extracts from a catalog merchant such as Sears & Roebuck or perhaps a door-to-door salesman for companies such as Watkins or Rawleigh's. Dairy products like sour cream, buttermilk, cream, milk, and butter would have been delivered fresh from the farm to those living in cities or small towns. Though the push was on to move to the city for an easier life, there were still plenty of small farm families who kept a milk cow and chickens to supply their family with needed meals in addition to great baking materials.

LIGHTNING CHURN

Yeah, sure, it's easier and cheaper to run to the supermarket for your baking ingredients, but if you're going to make historic cookies, go ahead and shop for the good stuff when you can. Here's what I recommend:

- **Locally farmed eggs**
- **Unsalted butter** (organic is nice, but pricey)
- **Unbleached white flour-** often organic markets will buy their flour from local mills. Support your hometown farmers! King Arthur and Hodgson Mills make good flours available in most groceries.
- **Locally milled whole wheat flour-** if possible, or the above commercial varieties are good as well.
- **Neighborhood honey-** if available
- **Homemade molasses-**if you can find it, but never bitter blackstrap.
- **Fresh spices-** replace yearly if not more often.
- **Real vanilla extract-** don't scrimp on this one.
- **Dried fruit and nuts-** purchased in bulk if possible. Organic raisins are about the same price as non-organic and taste MUCH better.
- **Seasalt-** supposedly makes a difference in baking.
- **Fresh baking powder and baking soda-** they go flat after a while.

SHORTENING

Baffled by the array of shortenings called for in Anna's cookie book? While fats didn't dominate vintage cookies as they seem to be doing now, shortening was the ingredient that mattered most in producing a good cookie. The baking fats of choice in the early 20th century included butter, cream, sour cream, lard, and "shortening," which was probably something like Crisco, Cottolene or oleomargarine.

Butter   Lard   Crisco

LARD

The best, called leaf lard, lies around the kidneys of the hog. According to the *Grocer's Encyclopedia*, 1911, "If pure, it should be white of the consistence of ointment and free from any disagreeable taste or smell." Lard had the advantage of being sold in tins and had a longer shelf-life than butter, so it was a good substitute when dairy shortenings were scarce. Lard produces a product with a slight pork flavor and lends a tender texture to baked goods that you can't get with butter.

WHITE SHORTENINGS

Crisco made its way into American pantries in 1911. At a time when butter was often rancid and lard imparted an undesirable pork flavor to food, solid shortenings made from vegetable oil touted to be "pure, white, and digestible" were a welcome relief to bakers. Fats like Crisco and Cottolene contained no water and stayed fresh unrefrigerated for long periods of time.

Oleomargarine was invented in 1871. It contained a mixture of beef tallow, leaf lard, butter or cream, and sometimes cottonseed oil. In order to protect dairy farmers, Congress passed a law in 1902 that levied a one-quarter cent tax per pound on uncolored margarine and ten cents per pound on the colored product. Some states forbid the product to be colored at all and it was to be plainly labeled so as not to be passed off for butter to unsuspecting consumers. I don't recommend you use these products in your cookies. They're bad for your health and they make a lousy Oat Crisp.

SHORTENING

TO MAKE BUTTER QUICKLY
White House Cook Book, 1887

Normally butter would have been made by allowing fresh milk to stand for 24-36 hours to ripen. The lightly fermented cream would have then been removed and churned into butter.

"Immediately after the cow is milked, strain the milk into clean pans, and set it over a moderate fire until it is scalding hot; do not let it boil; then set it aside; when it is cold, skim off the cream; the milk will still be fit for any ordinary use; when you have enough cream put it into a clean earthen basin; beat it with a wooden spoon until the butter is made, which will not be long; then take it from the milk and work it with a little cold water, until it is free from milk; then drain off the water, put a small tablespoonful of fine salt to each pound of butter and work it in. A small teaspoonful of fine white sugar, worked in with the salt, will be found an improvement—sugar is a great preservative. Make the butter in a roll; cover it with a bit of muslin and keep it in a cool place."

"Butter is indispensable in almost all culinary preparations. Good fresh butter, used in moderation, is easily digested; it is softening, nutritious and fattening, and is far more easily digested than any other of the oleaginous substances sometimes used in its place."

~*White House Cook Book, 1887*

Photo courtesy Florida State Archives

SHORTENING

BUTTER

Butter was the preferred shortening in Anna's day, and it's my favorite as well. *Domestic Science Principles,* 1924, instructs that "butter may be made from either sweet or ripened cream. Sweet-cream butter has a very delicate flavor and does not possess good keeping qualities because it is not salted. The ripening of the cream and the added salt give to butter a stronger flavor which is preferred by most persons and makes it better suited for marketing purposes." Who could have ever guessed folks would prefer the stronger flavor? The book goes on to add, "butter has the best color and flavor in the spring and summer when the cows are fed on fresh grass. The Guernsey breed produce butter of a naturally rich, yellow color."

We can assume that Anna used salted butter in her baking, but I recommend you bake with sweet, unsalted butter. Salted butter behaves differently than unsalted, and you'll be happier with the results you get from unsalted. Do add a good pinch of salt per stick of butter to compensate for the lack of salt in these recipes.

A Receipt for Cleansing Lard

Mrs. Winslow's Domestic Receipt Book, 1872

To five pounds lard take four good nice potatoes, pare, wash, and slice thin; put them in your lard as soon as hot; let them fry till brown; skim them out and pour out your lard to cool; it will be as sweet as when first tried out.

FLOUR

By the time 1917 rolled around, American cookie bakers were in good shape where flour was concerned. Bakers had their choice of prepackaged white, self-rising, graham (whole wheat), rye, barley, and rice flours. While white all-purpose flour was preferred for cookie baking, cooks made-do with less and substituted flours from other grains during World War I with some surprisingly good results.

For the most authentic and best-tasting old-fashioned cookies, always use unbleached all purpose flour, unless other flours are called for. All flours absorb liquids a little differently, so don't forget to make test cookies as you go along, especially when the recipes instructs you to "add flour to make a soft, or stiff dough."

This man was persuaded to buy another flour said to be as good as White Daisy flour, but he was fooled. He is now awake to the fact that he has been a loser.

This man uses White Daisy flour. It is made of good, clean wheat, and that makes pure, wholesome bread. His digestion is good and he is happy.

Payne's Self-Rising Flour Advertisement, 1890's

FLOUR

REMEMBER
How Your Mother Used To Do ?

Sprain her back and scrape against nails, burrowing on the bottom of a deep barrel.

Then she'd take the flour out, cupful at a time, pour it on the bread board and sift it; and sigh for an easier way of doing the work.

There wasn't any

CREAM CITY FLOUR BIN and SIFTER in those days,

IT'S HALF A BAKERY - This cream City Flour Bin. Holds the flour - sifts it, and puts just as much in the receptacle as you want. That's more than any other contrivance does.

The bottom's a sieve, and a reel sends the flour through as fine and fast as can be. Over the reel is a shield which keeps the weight off, and the crank from clogging. Under the sieve is a convenient pan that catches every speck of the down-coming flour.

It works like a charm, doesn't take up much space and is really ornamental. Just think how much more so than a bulky barrel or leaky sack!

There Ought to be One in Your Kitchen

It will do away with no end of back-aches, belated meals and the like.

SWEETENERS

Molasses, brown and white sugar, and honey sweetened cookies in 1917, just as these substances do now, but with one big difference. The American per capita consumption of sugar in 1911 was 82 pounds. In 2000, we gobbled an average of 152 pounds of caloric sweeteners per person. Our modern monster-sized, overly sweet, and fat-laden gunky cookies would make Anna quake in her pumps. When you oversweeten a baked good, you miss out on the subtle flavors of butter, nuts, and spices, for all you taste is the sugar. Resist the temptation to double the sugar in these not-too-sweet cookie recipes, because that not only covers up flavor, but also changes the texture as well. Anna's older recipes for sugar, ginger, and molasses cookies could use an extra dab of sugar; just keep in mind that increasing sweeteners causes cookies to spread when baking and brown more quickly.

Molasses is the one sweetener liberally called for in these recipes that you will need to inform yourself about. The first thing you need to know is that here in the Appalachian mountains, where they're still being made, molasses are plural. As in "These molasses taste really good," or "The molasses are almost finished cooking."

The *Grocer's Encyclopedia*, 1911, describes molasses as "the mother water that is separated from the crystals of raw sugar during the manufacture of sugar. Sugar cane juice is condensed into syrup, then the uncrystallizable syrup is spun off and sold as molasses. The best grades are of bright amber tint." This includes molasses made in Louisiana, known as New Orleans molasses, that you'll recognize as the recommended brand in these pages. Steer clear of "blackstrap" molasses. It was an inferior product in 1911, and it still is. It's a tar-colored, bitter, reboiled molasses that's low in taste as well as nutrients.

Here in the North Carolina mountains, folks are still making molasses that are as tasty today as they were 150 years ago. Sugar cane or sorghum stalks are fed through a cane mill where the juice is extracted, then it's strained and poured into a long shallow boiling pan that sits overtop a wood fired furnace. Sixty gallons of juice will make just one gallon of molasses, and the boiling and stirring and skimming goes on all day long. The molasses are ready when they turn a deep golden brown color and the boiling bubbles look like "frog eyes." That's about when you run into the house and make a big pan of biscuits!

MOLASSES

Anytime you see a quart jar of homemade molasses, grab it. It'll keep on your shelf for years, but it's so tasty and good for you, you'll eat it in no time. For cookie baking, try out your recipe with store-bought varieties (Grandma's is a good one), and after you perfect it, then use your precious homemade molasses for baking.

Courtesy NC Archives and History

Feeding the sorghum cane through the cane mill

Courtesy Great Smoky Mtns. Nat. Park

Stirring the boiling molasses syrup

LEAVENING

W hat a deal it must have been getting cookies to rise in Anna's day. Half her recipes were mid-to late-19th century in origin when adulterated leavening was the order of the day, while many others reflected adaptations due to World War I egg shortages. I'm no baking expert, but there doesn't seem to be much consistency on what and how much of which chemical raises what cookie in Anna's book. The exception is with acid-containing cookie ingredients, where you will always find baking soda, in varying amounts, as the leavening agent.

In fact, Mother's Cookie, no. 190 on page 39, calls for baking soda, cream of tartar, and baking powder. Just throw 'em all in and hope one works! Generally, there seems to be too much baking powder called for in these recipes, compared to the amount we use today. I wouldn't get too worked up about funky leavening suggestions, we're not trying to be pastry chefs or anything. Just having a little historical fun. In general:

½ **tsp. soda per 1 cup sour milk**
¼ **tsp. soda per cup of flour**
1 **tsp. soda per 1 cup molasses**
½-1 **tsp. baking powder for each cup of flour (I prefer ½)**
¼ **tsp. soda + ½ tsp. cream of tartar= 1 tsp. baking powder.**

The O. K. Shaker Sifter

For Soda Recipes, 1915

When using sour milk recipes which call for soda in the baking, try using one fourth spoonful of soda and one spoonful of baking powder instead of each spoonful of soda called for. You will be delighted with the result. The food will be lighter and there will be no taste of the soda.   *~ The Modern Priscilla*

LEAVENING

Baking Soda: When baking soda (an alkali) is combined with an acid ingredient like buttermilk or molasses, carbon dioxide bubbles are formed and the product rises. As soon you get these guys together (soda + acid), bubbles start happening, so you need to keep the dry ingredients together as you mix, and work quickly to get the cookies in the oven. Theoretically, that is. I'm never in that much of a hurry and the cookies seem to rise anyway.

Baking Powder is a combination of sodium bicarbonate and an acid. When moisture and heat combine with the product, carbon dioxide is formed. Double acting baking powders contain a couple of kinds of acids; one reacts with the moisture in the bowl and the other finishes the leavening job with the heat of the oven. Many 19th century recipes called for baking soda plus cream of tartar (an acid), which did the job of puffing cookies but with less of the rising that takes place at higher temperatures. This is still an acceptable form of leavening for cookies.

19th Century Leaveners

Pearlash, or potassium carbonate, was a product made from leaching the lye out of wood ashes. When you combine lye with fat, guess what you get? Soap. Now, I don't know if pearlash cookies tasted of soap, but the product was replaced by saleratus by the 1840's.

Saleratus was a more refined, but still bitter, version of pearlash. It contained either potassium bicarbonate or sodium bicarbonate. Eventually, sodium bicarbonate would be made from plant and mineral sources resulting in a baking soda that had a more palatable flavor. Most recipes recorded during the last couple of decades of the 19th century that call for saleratus are actually referring to baking soda.

Tartaric acid, the forerunner of cream of tartar, was a by-product of the fermentation of wine. The acid, in combination with bicarbonate of soda, formed baking powder, which became commercially available in the 1850's.

Hartshorn is ammonium bicarbonate, known as baking ammonia. It's often called for in Springerle cookies and is still available. I hear it creates a stinky dough, but produces a very light, crisp cookie supposedly with no telltale ammonia taste when baked.

THE RANGE

What an exciting time to be baking cookies! With a choice between ranges powered by electricity, wood, coal, gas, or combinations of coal, wood and gas, how could a housewife decide which stove to buy in 1917? My guess is that it depended on where you lived. If you lived on a farm, you would have used a wood or coal - fired cook-stove.

Here's a Home Comfort wood cook-stove with the firebox to the left of the oven and water jacket on the far left. You'd load the wood through the top of the front left burner. Note the warming ovens above for keeping foods hot. To bake, you'd get some good embers glowing and close the damper in the flu so hot air circulated around the ovenbox. Cookies had to be turned around in the oven so they didn't get overbaked on the left-hand side next to the fire. I'm in love with wood cook-stoves. We have a 1928 Home Comfort that'll turn out a dandy batch of gingerbread cookies.

"Built to Bake"

If you lived in a small town or a city as Anna probably did, you would have been using gas to cook with in the late 1910's. The first gas ranges for home use were introduced in the 1880's. This one uses coal on the left and gas on the right; especially convenient if your town was just making gas available to area residents. You'd think this Household Liberty stove would be "built to blow up," but the manufacturer claimed you could use both sides at once.

THE RANGE

The first electric range was manufactured by Hotpoint in 1910. Wasn't it a dandy? All you needed was electricity. Only 13% of American farm families had electric power in 1930. It wasn't until the passing of the Rural Electrification Act of 1936 that ranges such as this would be available to rural households. While urban homes were being wired for electricity in the early part of the 20th century, electric ranges wouldn't be common in household kitchens until the 1920's.

OVEN TEMPERATURE

If the oven temperatures in Anna's book seem vexing, that's because baking temperature was an inexact science, at best, during her day. Here's how the Majestic Range company suggested you control the temperature in about 1910: *"If a quick oven is desired, open the drought door in front under the fire door. If a slow, gradual heat is wanted, close and operate slide as required."* For the rest of us, here is an approximate guide to baking instructions found in this book:

Slow oven: 300-325°
Moderate oven: 350°
Moderately hot oven: 375°
Hot or quick oven: 400°-450°

REFRIGERATION

Come over here and let's peek into Anna's zinc-lined insulated oak icebox. Today the ice man delivered a big old block of ice, and the butter, milk, and cream are nicely chilled. But is there any cookie dough in there? Does she ever get tired of cutting out cookies and think to cover a roll of dough in some waxed paper to slice and bake for later? Probably not.

Icebox cookies didn't show up in cookbooks until electric refrigerators appeared in American households beginning in about 1928. You will only see one recipe of Anna's in this book that suggests you chill the dough before rolling it, in order to make it easier to handle (no. 220 pg. 105). The cookie queen probably didn't need to do anything to make her dough easier to work, but for you and me, the modern refrigerator can do wonders to tame those sticky Jumbles.

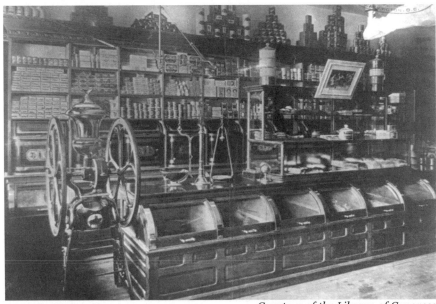

Courtesy of the Library of Congress

PACKAGED GOODS

SHALL THE HOUSEKEEPER USE PACKAGE GOODS?
NEW LIGHT ON A MUCH DISCUSSED SUBJECT
by Winnifred Harper Cooley
Modern Priscilla Magazine, January, 1915

"I can see in imagination the old-fashioned, corner grocery store of my childhood, which had the extensive patronage of a respectable, intelligent, well-to-do neighborhood.

There was the filthy hogshead of brine, with miscellaneous herring, cheap fish, or pickles. There was the kerosene in close proximity to the butter. There was the cat, reposing on the sugar-barrel, and the mice scurrying away from the open bin of crackers. All kinds of meal and flour were exposed in open boxes, barrels and vats. In the window were miscellaneous cheap candies, pies, open jams, bulk apple butter, all swarming with flies.

Contrast this picture with the modern exquisitely kept "dry grocery," upon whose shelves and in whose windows are rows upon rows, and pyramids and tiers of neat, clean, bright packages.

The instance of sugar is especially interesting. It is only today that granulated sugar is being put into two pound pasteboard boxes, instead of being scooped up with a wooden shovel from the grocer's barrel. The housekeeper has been bombarded with arguments in behalf of this final innovation, and it seems as though the last barrier of prejudice against dry food in packages has been broken down."

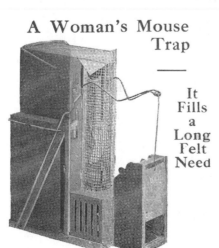

A Woman's Mouse Trap

—

It Fills a Long Felt Need

We call this *"a woman's mouse trap"* because it is the most satisfactory one ever made for a woman's use. The mouse walks into the front door, closes and locks the door behind him, walks upstairs and promptly drowns himself in a tank of water at the back of the trap. He can't help himself. All the bother of taking a live mouse out of the trap is done away with. If you are troubled with mice, get one of these traps and be happy. Given as payment for securing 4 new subscriptions for *The Modern Priscilla.*

The Modern Priscilla, October, 1909

TEA TIME

What will you drink with your cookies?
Coffee, tea, or milk?

In making coffee observe that the broader the bottom and the smaller the top of the vessel the better the coffee will be. Never let coffee or tea stand in tin.   Sloan's Handy Hints and Up-to-Date Cook Book, 1901

Courtesy of the Library of Congress

JUMBLES

Jumbles, known also as Jumbals or Gemmels, were popular ring-shaped cookies in England and other neighboring European countries in the 17th and 18th centuries. Since coming to America, the cookies have changed over time from hard-baked, rolled out strands of intertwined dough, to a more tender rolled cookie with a hole cut out of the middle. Early Jumbles were made with only butter, sugar, eggs, flour and were often flavored with rosewater or caraway seeds. As you look at Anna's Jumble recipes, you can see the progression from the English version of this ring-shaped cookie to something that looks just like what we would now consider a regular sugar cookie.

65. BUFFALO JUMBLES OR COOKIES

4 eggs, 2 cups sugar, 1 cup butter, 1 teaspoon soda, 1 teaspoon lemon extract. Add flour enough to make a soft dough. Roll very thin, (handle as little as possible) cut in rounds then with thimble cut out center. Bake in hot oven.

88. SOFT JUMBLES COOKIE

⅔ cup butter, 1 cup sugar, 3 eggs, 1 cup milk, 2 teaspoons baking powder, 3 cups flour, grated rind of 1 lemon. Drop by teaspoon on greased pan & bake until golden brown.

96. LEMON JUMBLES COOKIES

1 egg, 1 cup sugar, ½ cup butter, 3 teaspoons milk, 2 teaspoons baking powder, flavor with lemon. Add enough flour to mix stiff, cut thin.

99. JUMBLE COOKIES

1 cup butter, 1 cup sugar, 4 eggs, 2 cups flour, 1 teaspoon baking powder. Mix all, flour the board & roll out the dough rather thin. Cut with jumble cutter or cookie cutter & cut center out with thimble & bake in fairly hot oven 10 minutes.

JUMBLES

WINE JUMBLES
White House Cook Book, 1887

Like to get your holiday baking done ahead of time? Will this do?

"One cup of butter, two of sugar, three eggs, one wine-glass of wine, one spoonful of vanilla and flour enough to roll out. Roll as thin as the blade of a knife and cut with an oval cutter. Bake on tin-sheets in a quick oven until a dark brown. **These will keep a year if kept in a tin box and in a dry place.**"

JELLY JUMBLES
Boston Cooking-School Cook Book, 1918

Many of Anna's recipes came from the 1906 and later versions of Fannie Farmer's Cook Book. This is the same recipe as Anna's no. 14, Sour Milk Soft Cookies on pg. 34, but Miss Farmer suggests you chill the dough before rolling and add currant jelly, which goes great with any sugar cookie. Make as a sandwich cookie as instructed below or just punch your thumb into a ball of sugar cookie dough and fill with a small amount of jelly before baking.

½ cup butter	1 egg
½ cup sour milk	Flour
1 cup sugar	½ tsp. soda
¼ teaspoon salt	Currant jelly

Cream the butter, add sugar gradually, egg well beaten, soda mixed with milk, salt and flour to make a soft dough. Chill and shape, using a round cutter. On the centres of one-half the pieces put currant jelly. Make three small openings in remaining halves, using a thimble, and put pieces together. Press edges slightly, and bake in a rather hot oven, that jumbles may keep in good shape.

JUMBLES

100. JUMBLES

1½ cups butter, 2 cups sugar, 6 eggs, 1½ pints flour, ½ cup corn starch, 1 teaspoon baking powder, 1 teaspoon extract lemon, ½ cup chopped peanuts mixed with ½ cup granulated sugar. Roll the dough out rather thin, cut with cookie cutter & bake 8 to 10 minutes.

114. RING JUMBLES OR DROP COOKIES

1 lb. butter, 1 lb. sugar, 4 eggs, 1 lb. flour, or enough to make a soft dough, 3 teaspoons extract of rose. Mix all together, adding the well beaten whites of eggs last. Line shallow baking sheet with buttered paper. With a spoon form rings of the dough & bake quickly & sift fine sugar over them as soon as you take them out from the oven.

Mary Randolph published an almost identical recipe in her 1824 cookbook, *The Virginia House-wife*. Here it is:

To Make Jumbals

To one pound of butter and one of flour, add one pound of sugar, four eggs beaten light, and whatever spice you like; knead all well together, and bake it nicely.

Also, try this recipe for **Chocolate Jumbles** from the 1911, *Inglenook Cook Book*. Just for fun, you can intertwine ropes of chocolate along with the vanilla dough.

Take 2 cups of sugar, 1 cup of butter, 1 cup of grated chocolate, 4 eggs, 1 teaspoon of soda, 1 teaspoon of cream of tartar, and 3 cups of flour. Roll thin and cut in any pattern desired.

SUGAR COOKIES

I n a minute, you'll be asking yourself, "Just how many sour cream cookie recipes that look almost exactly the same does one person need?" Not this many, I can assure you. Unless, of course, you are a recipe-collecting, cookie-baking queen. Then you need ALL of them, and so, that's just what we have here. Every single sour cream, buttermilk, and milk-based sugar cookie in existence in 1918. Don't even get me started on the molasses/ginger cookies!

These cookies are leavened with baking soda combined with acid from the sour cream or buttermilk. They are pretty much soft, puffy, rolled, and not very sweet or exciting cookies. But they are old-fashioned and just the kind of cookie you'd whip up if you had fresh cream in your springbox and a bunch of hungry youngsters needing a hearty afternoon snack.

14. SOUR MILK SOFT COOKIES
½ cup butter, ½ cup sour milk, 1½ cup sugar, ½ teaspoon soda, ¼ teaspoon cream of tartar, 1 egg, vanilla, flour to roll, roll rather thick.

20. PLAIN COOKIES
2 cups sugar, ¾ cup lard, 1 cup buttermilk, (or) sour milk. 1 teaspoon each of soda & cream of tartar, & flour to make a stiff dough. Any flavoring may be used. I like 1 teaspoon nutmeg. Press a flattened raisin in center of each cookie.

21. SOUR MILK COOKIES
1 cup each of sour milk, & gra. sugar, 1 egg, ¼ cup melted lard, 2 teaspoons baking powder, ½ teaspoon soda, pinch salt, 1 teaspoon nutmeg, flour enough to make a soft dough to roll. Cut & bake in quick oven to a nice brown.

SUGAR COOKIES

29. SOUR CREAM DROP COOKIES

1 cup sour cream, 1 cup sugar, 2 ½ cups flour, 1 egg, ½ teaspoon salt, 1 level teaspoon soda, (dissolved in a little hot water), & 1 teaspoon baking powder. Sifted flour.

39. EGGLESS COOKIES

1 cup sugar, 1 cup thick sour cream, 1 teaspoon soda dissolved in a little hot water, pinch salt, flavor to taste, flour to roll.

45. FAIRY COOKIES

2 cups sugar, ½ cup butter, 2 eggs, 1 cup sour cream in which dissolve 1 teaspoon soda. Flavor with 1 teaspoon of lemon or vanilla, add enough flour to make a soft dough. Keep dough in a cool place, rolling out but one baking at a time. Roll out thin, sprinkle with colard (sic) sugar. Cut with cookie cutter. Put a flattened raisin in center of each cookie & bake in a moderate oven not too hot as they should not brown.

74. CREAM DROP COOKIES

Measure 2 big cups flour, pinch salt, ¾ teaspoon soda, ⅔ teaspoon cream of tartar. Sift all in mixing bowl, now stir in 1 cup sour cream, 1 egg, & beat to a smooth batter that will drop from spoon. Bake in quick oven 20 minutes.

77. COOKIES

1 ½ cup sugar, ½ cup butter, 3 eggs, 1 cup sour cream, ½ teaspoon soda, 1 teaspoon cream of tartar. Mix soft, roll quite thick, lay well apart so they do not touch & bake.

SUGAR COOKIES

86. SOUR MILK COOKIES

Mix ½ cup butter, 1 cup sugar, 2 eggs, 1 cup sour milk & 1 teaspoon soda in 2 cups flour & 1 teaspoon scant baking powder. Then add enough flour to roll soft ¼ inch thick. Cut & put a raisin in center of each cookie & bake.

125. DROP COOKIES

Cream together: 1 cup sugar, 1 tablespoon shortning (melted), yokes of 2 eggs. Add 1 cup sour milk, with ½ teaspoon soda dissolved in spoonful of lukewarm water. Mix all together, add 2½ cups flour, last the beaten whites of 2 eggs. Flavor with vanilla or lemon. Drop with spoon on greased, flour dusted cookie pans & bake in slow oven.

126. COOKIES PLAIN

2 eggs, 1 cup sugar, 1 cup butter, 1 cup sour cream, 1 teaspoon soda, flour enough to roll out. Flavor with lemon or any flavoring.

129. FANCY COOKIES

Mix 2 cups brown sugar, 1 cup shortning, 2 eggs, ½ cup sour cream or milk, pinch salt, ½ scant teaspoon of nutmeg, & 4 tablespoons of warm water in which dissolve ½ teaspoon soda. Flour enough to roll out. You can make different shape cookies out of this dough. Wash some with milk & sprinkle with colored course sugar. Others sprinkle with currants & some with cocoanut. Bake in slow oven.

132. SOUR CREAM COOKIES

1½ cups sugar, 2 cups sour cream, 2 level teaspoons soda, 2 eggs, 2 teaspoons extract of lemon, pinch salt. Flour enough to roll out soft. Bake in quick oven.

SUGAR COOKIES

150. SUGAR COOKIES

2 cups sugar, 2 eggs, 1 cup shortening, 1 cup buttermilk (or sour milk), 1 teaspoon soda, pinch salt, flavor to taste, flour enough to roll. Cut & bake in quick oven. These are very good.

152. WHITE SUGAR COOKIES

1 cup sugar, 4½ cups flour, 2 teaspoons baking powder. 1 cup lard, 2 eggs, ½ cup sour milk, ½ teaspoon soda, pinch of salt, 1 teaspoon of nutmeg. Mix soft, roll out, cut & bake in quick oven.

156. SOFT COOKIES

1 big cup butter, 1 cup sugar, 2 eggs, whites & yokes beaten separately, 3 tablespoons sour milk, 1 small teaspoon soda (dissolved) & as little flour as will make them stiff enough to roll. Sprinkle with sugar & nutmeg. Bake light brown.

Nutmeg Grater, 1906

Does not clog nor tear the fingers, nor drop the nutmeg, very simple, nicely finished.

180. CREAM COOKIES

Cream ½ cup butter with 1½ cups sugar, add 1 egg & beat until very light, 1 cup sour cream, with 1 teaspoon soda in it, 1 tablespoon vanilla & flour enough to roll. Bake in a quick oven to light brown.

211. CREAM COOKIES

Cream ½ cup butter, 1½ cups sugar, 1 egg, 1 cup sour cream in which dissolve 1 teaspoon soda, 1 teaspoon vanilla & enough flour to roll. Bake in quick oven to a delicate brown.

SUGAR COOKIES

This next group of sugar cookies is made with sweet milk. Notice that baking powder is the leavening agent.

76. QUICK COOKIES

1 cup butter, 1½ cups sugar, 1 cup sweet milk, 5 cups flour, 3 tablespoons baking powder & 1 teaspoon cinnamon or any other flavoring liked.

84. PLAIN COOKIES

½ cup butter, 1 cup sugar, ½ teaspoon nutmeg, 1 egg, 3½ cups flour, 3 teaspoons baking powder, ½ cup milk. Roll ½ inch thick, dredge with sugar & bake in a moderate oven.

85. WHITE COOKIES

2 cups sugar, ½ cup butter, 2 eggs, 1 cup sweet milk, 3 teaspoons baking powder, flavor with lemon extract & add enough flour to roll.

SUGAR COOKIES

93. COOKIES

2 cups sugar, 1 of butter, ¾ cup sweet milk, 2 eggs, 5 cups flour, 2 teaspoons baking powder, roll thin & bake quickly. Caraway seeds may be added.

106. SUGAR COOKIES

1 cup sugar, ¾ cup butter, ¼ cup sweet milk, 2 eggs, 3 teaspoons baking powder, pinch salt, ½ teaspoon extract of cinnamon. Flour enough to roll. Cut cookies, sprinkle with course sugar, & bake in a quick oven.

Courtesy of the Library of Congress

190. MOTHERS COOKIES

½ cup butter, 2 cups light brown sugar, 1 egg & beat well. Then add 6 tablespoons sweet milk, 2½ cups flour mixed with 1 teaspoon each of cinnamon, cream of tartar, ½ teaspoon soda & baking powder, & pinch salt. Drop from spoon & bake in quick oven.

Mother was not about to take any chances having her very sweet cookies turn out flat. Covering all her bases, she added every possible leavening agent available: cream of tartar, baking powder, soda, and an egg!

SUGAR COOKIES

103. ROYAL COOKIES

1 cup butter, 2 cups sugar, 5 eggs, 1½ pints flour, 1 teaspoon baking powder, 1 cup milk. Mix butter, sugar, & eggs smooth; add flour sifted with powder & milk. Mix into a dough soft enough to handle conveniently. Flour the board, roll out dough thin. Cut cookies & bake in hot oven 5 or 6 minutes.

*Recipe comes from *Royal Baking Powder Cook Book,* 1911.

204. ROYAL COOKIES #2

1 cup butter, 2 cups sugar, 5 eggs, 1½ pints flour, 2½ teaspoons baking powder, 1 cup milk. Mix butter, sugar & eggs smooth. Add flour sifted with powder then milk. Mix into soft dough to handle conveniently. Flour the board, roll out dough thin. Cut & bake.

*Same as previous Royal cookies, only more baking powder.

111. BEST COOKIES

2 cups powdered sugar, ½ cup butter, 1 cup sweet milk, whites of 4 eggs, 1 teaspoon extract of lemon, 2 teaspoons baking powder, flour enough to make a stiff batter. Drop from spoon. When cold ice with soft white icing made with whites of 4 eggs & powdered sugar enough to make them stiff.

*Try these and see if you don't think they taste exactly like **animal crackers**! Use a royal icing recipe to frost cookies, but use powdered egg white because fresh uncooked egg whites can make you very sick (if contaminated by Salmonella bacteria).

116. IRENE'S LIGHT COOKIES

2 eggs, 2 cups granulated sugar, 1 liberal cup lard, ⅔ cup sweet milk, 1 teaspoon nutmeg, pinch of salt, 2 heaping teaspoons baking powder, sifted with flour. Mix soft & roll quite thick.

Mrs. Stewart, Snohomish Wash.

Sugar Cookies

120. Dew Drops

2 cups powdered sugar, ½ cup butter, 1 cup sweet milk, whites of 4 eggs, 1 teaspoon extract of lemon, 2 teaspoons baking powder, & flour enough to make a soft batter. Bake in patty tins & ice when cold (or make stiff batter & drop cookies on greased tin). Bake in quick oven.

153. Sugar Cookies

1 cup sugar, ½ cup lard, 2 eggs, 1 teaspoon salt, ½ cup sweet milk, 2 teaspoons baking powder sifted with enough flour to mix soft. Flavor to taste, roll thin & sprinkle with sugar.

155. Plain Cookies

2 cups sugar, 1 cup butter, ¾ cup sweet milk, 2 eggs, 5 cups flour, 2 teaspoons baking powder. Roll thin & bake quickly.

163. Sponge Cookies

1 cup sugar, 2 eggs, 2 teaspoons baking powder (rounding), pinch salt, 2 teaspoons lemon juice or 1 teaspoon vanilla, ½ cup shortning & ½ cup sweet milk. Flour enough to roll soft. Handle as little as possible. Bake in quick oven.

197. Plain Cookies

½ cup butter, 1½ cups sugar, 2 beaten eggs, 1 cup water or sweet milk, 1 teaspoon nutmeg, 1 cup flour sifted with 1 teaspoon baking powder, pinch salt, and sufficient flour to make soft dough. Roll out cut into cookies & bake pale brown in moderate oven.

SUGAR COOKIES

83. ROCK COOKIES

6 tablespoons butter, 1 cup sugar, 3 eggs, 4 cups flour, pinch salt, 2 teaspoons baking powder. Mix as usual & bake in quick oven.

89. LADY FINGERS COOKIES

Beat 2 eggs, 1 cup sugar, pinch salt, flavor to taste, 1 cup flour, 1 teaspoon baking powder. Roll out & cut into strips the size of finger & bake. Must use enough more flour to roll this out.

Courtesy of University of Louisville

94. THIN RICH COOKIES

1 cup butter, 1 cup sugar, 3 eggs, 2 teaspoons baking powder. Use only enough flour to mix & roll thin. Flavor to taste, cut & bake quickly.

Sugar Cookies

154. Shingles Square Cookie

1 cup butter, 1½ cups sugar, 2 eggs, 4 cups flour mixed with 2 teaspoons baking powder. Roll very thin & cut squares. Sprinkle tops with sugar.

162. Sand Tart Cookies

1 cup butter, 1½ cups sugar, 3 eggs (whites & yelks beaten separately), 1 tablespoon milk, 2 teaspoons baking powder. Flour enough to roll. Roll out thin, sprinkle sugar & cinnamon on top.
Author's note: "Yelk" is an old-timey word for "yolk."

166. Plain Cookies

Mix ⅔ cup butter, 1½ cups sugar, 3 eggs, 1½ cups flour & 2 teaspoons baking powder, 2 tablespoons milk. Roll out thin & cut.

Fire Superstitions 1898

If you go to light a match and strike the wrong end, it is a sure sign of disappointment in love.

When the sparks fly out of the fire, a maiden may expect a call from her sweetheart.

If a coal of fire falls on the floor, it is a sign of a stranger coming to see you.

SUGAR COOKIES

195. SOFT COOKIES

1 cup butter, 1½ cups sugar, 2 eggs, 3 tablespoons milk,
1 teaspoon baking powder, just enough flour to roll out
to a soft dough. Sprinkle with sugar, cut in rounds &
bake in quick oven.

208. BLITZ KITCHEN: A COOKIE

3 cups sugar, 3 cups flour, 1 cup butter, 6 eggs, chopped
nuts any kind to suit. Spread the batter very thin, so
thin that you can see the bottom of the tins. Sprinkle
with sugar & cinnamon & cut into squares immediately
when baked. Or drop small spoonfuls far apart in pan
& bake.

Courtesy of the Library of Congress

*Grease the underside of the spout of your cream pitcher with butter
and the cream will not run down the side of the pitcher.*
                              ~Dr. Miles Hints to Housekeepers, 1920

SUGAR COOKIES

173 & 201. SAND TARTS

1 cup butter, 1½ cups sugar, 3 eggs, 1 tablespoon water, ½ teaspoon baking powder, & flour enough to roll out. Cut in squares & sprinkle with gra. sugar & powdered cinnamon before baking in hot oven.

Danderine

Grows Hair and we can **PROVE IT!**

Several of Anna's recipes came from Comfort magazine. Here's an advertisement from the May, 1910 issue.

Roll this dough into balls and dredge with cinnamon sugar before baking, and you get Snickerdoodles. Crunchy on the outside and soft on the inside, this simple favorite cookie has appeared in American cookbooks since the 1930's. The use of soda along with cream of tartar for leavening was common practice during the mid-19th century before baking powder became widely available. I'm betting that some creative New England cookie baker took an old sand tart recipe and livened it up with a new shape and the perky name of Snickerdoodle. Here's the traditional recipe. I found this in a little homemade Ladies Aid cookie notebook from the 1950's.

SNICKERDOODLES

Mix together thoroughly:
> **1 cup soft shortening (butter)**
> **1½ cup sugar**
> **2 eggs**

Sift together and stir in:
> **2¾ cup sifted flour (use less if you don't sift)**
> **2 tsp. cream of tartar**
> **1 tsp. soda**
> **½ tsp. salt**

Chill dough. Roll into small balls, then roll in mixture of 2 Tbs. sugar and 2 tsp. cinnamon. Place 2 inches apart on ungreased cookie sheet and flatten just a tiny bit. Bake at 400° for 8-10 minutes. Don't overbake, they should be crisp outside and soft inside.

SUGAR COOKIES

SAND TARTS
The People's Home Journal, March 1907

"Beat one-half pound of butter to a cream and add one-half pound of granulated sugar; then add the yolks of three eggs and the whites of two, beaten together; add one teaspoonful of vanilla and just a little grated nutmeg. Mix in sufficient flour to make a dough. Dust your baking board thickly with granulated sugar. Take out a piece of dough, roll it into a thin sheet, cut with round cutters and bake in a moderate oven until a light brown. Dust the top of the sheet with sugar instead of flour, to prevent the roller from sticking. By adding one-half pound of cleaned currants to the above recipe you will have Shrewsbury currant cakes."

Welsh Cakes in a Wales bakery window

SHREWSBURY CAKES

You don't have to wonder where Shrewsbury Cakes came from. The rich scalloped edged round biscuits have been enjoyed in the British town of Shrewsbury for hundreds of years. I found this recipe in a used book shop in the famous book town of Hay-On-Wye in Wales. Across the street was a bakery with some beautiful piles of Welsh Cakes. They've a long tradition in Wales and contain similar ingredients in different proportions as Shrewsbury Cakes, only they are baked on a girdle (iron griddle) instead of in an oven.

½ cup butter	2 egg yolks
⅔ cup sugar	1½ cup flour
Grated lemon rind	½ cup currants

Cream butter and sugar, then add egg yolks and beat. Stir in the flour, lemon rind, and currants. Turn out onto a floured board and knead lightly. Roll out about ¼ inch thick, and cut with a round 2-inch cutter. Bake about 12 minutes at 350° until light brown.

CITRUS SUGAR COOKIES

105. LEMON COOKIES

Beat 6 eggs; whites & yolkes separately. 1 cup butter, 3 small cups sugar, 2 teaspoon extract lemon. Flour enough to make a soft dough to mold. Roll thin & bake in quick oven.

87. LEMON SNAP COOKIES

1 cup sugar, ½ cup butter, 2 eggs, 1 teaspoon extract lemon, ½ teaspoon soda dissolved in 1 tablespoon sour milk. Flour enough to roll soft & roll very thin.

157. ORANGE THIN, RICH COOKIES

1 cup butter, 1 cup sugar, 3 eggs, 2 teaspoons of baking powder, 3 teaspoons extract orange, flour enough to mix soft, roll thin (use no milk or water). Bake quickly.

205. ORANGE COOKIES

2 cups sugar, 1 cup butter, 1 egg, juice & grated rind of 1 orange, 1 cup sour milk, 1 teaspoon soda, pinch salt. Stir all well together and add enough flour with 1 teaspoon baking powder to make a soft dough to roll. Cut & bake in quick oven.

SHORTBREAD COOKIES

What could be easier to make than a cookie made from just butter, flour, and sugar? After going through about 5 pounds of butter with some rather disappointing results, I'd say anything could be easier. Not one to give up easily, I decided a Scottish baker would have to teach me how to make this traditional biscuit. So on a recent vacation to the United Kingdom, I ate (in the name of research, of course) enough shortbread cookies to clog something I probably need. When I found the best ones at a small flea market, I begged the Scottish baker for her secret. Turns out she insisted she didn't have a secret. Same old recipe you find in every cookbook. 4 oz. butter, 2 oz. caster sugar, 6 oz. flour and a little ground rice flour. That's it. Bake at mark 4 on a gas range or 350° until pale brown.

Wouldn't you know there IS a secret. It's in the European cows. Their cream has a higher fat content than that of their American cousins. Our pale yellow grocery store butters with all kinds of additives don't make the very best shortbreads. Organic butters from grass-eating cows are OK, but you'll find that splurging on European butter, widely available at specialty markets, makes all the difference in the world.

Your choice of flour matters too. The Scottish add a bit of rice flour for crunch. Unbleached flour will also produce a firmer cookie, and chilling the dough before rolling keeps cookies from spreading while baking. It's easy to make small batches while you're practicing the art of shortbread baking.

TRADITIONAL SCOTTISH PETTICOAT TAILS

2 cups flour	**½ cup confectioners sugar**
1 cup butter	**¼ cup rice flour**

Cream butter and sugar. Sift in flours and work into a smooth dough with fingers. Divide into two balls. Roll out each ball to about ½ inch thick. Place both rounds on a greased cookie sheet. Prick all over with a fork. If you're feeling fancy, you can crimp the outer edges a bit. Mark each round into 6 triangles. Bake at 350° about 20 minutes until just barely very light brown. While warm, cut into triangles, and cool before packing into an airtight tin.

A Genuine Scotch Short Bread

An Old Recipe brought up to date.

1 *pound of Flour.*
1-4 " *of Powdered Sugar.*
1-4 " *of Butter.*
1-4 " *of Cottolene.*

Mix thoroughly with the hands ; form in a flat cake one inch thick ; quarter with a sharp knife ; bake in a slow oven until a delicate brown. The old way was good but the new is better.

Cottolene

196. COCOANUT COOKIES

1 cup butter, 2 cups sugar, 1 cup grated cocoanut, 1 teaspoon vanilla, 2 teaspoons baking powder, flour to roll out. Bake pale brown.

This is either a coconut shortbread, or Anna forgot the eggs and milk found in most of her recipes. As a shortbread, these are way too sweet, but with a few minor adjustments, you can make a dandy cookie.

1 cup butter	**1 tsp. vanilla**
¾ cup sugar	**2 cups flour**
Pinch salt	**¼ tsp. baking powder**
1 cup unsweetened coconut	

To mix and bake, follow the directions for shortbread cookies on the following page.

•*When working in pastry, never cut the dough with a knife or you will never be rich.*
•*When seasoning with salt, always take a little more than you need and put the rest back, so you will never want.*

~*Home Secrets, 1898*

SHORTBREAD COOKIES

171. SCOTCH COOKIES (VERY RICH)

Mix 1 lb. flour, ½ teaspoon baking powder, rub in ½ lb. butter (as for biscuits). Work in ⅔ cup sugar, 1 teaspoon extract of vanilla. This makes a crumbly dough. Now work with hand to make it adhere. Pat out in cakes, sprinkle with caraway seed. Bake in moderate oven.

SHORTBREAD COOKIES

This is my version based on making 25 different recipes of shortbread cookies and eating about 8 pounds of butter in the process.

½ cup softened unsalted butter
⅓ cup confectioners or superfine sugar or some of each
1 cup unbleached flour
⅛ cup rice flour (available at Asian markets)
Pinch salt (optional)
½ tsp. vanilla

Cream butter and sugar, add vanilla. Sift flours and salt and blend with hands until mixture is crumbly. Form into a flattened ball, wrap in plastic wrap, and chill about 30 minutes. Roll out ½ inch thick and cut with small circle cutter or cut into fingers. Prick each cookie several times with a fork all the way through. Bake in a preheated 325° oven on an ungreased cookie sheet for about 15 minutes or until barely light brown. Cool and store in an airtight container until teatime.

Brandied Cherry Shortbreads: Chop up a handful of dried sour cherries and soak them in brandy until plump before adding to dough.
Butterscotch Pecan Shortbreads: Use brown sugar instead of confectioner's and add a handful of chopped, toasted pecans to the dough.
Rosemary Shortbreads: This amazingly delicious 19th century crunchy, buttery cookie has just a hint of rosemary and is beautiful as well. Just mix 1 teaspoon finely chopped fresh (a must) rosemary in with other ingredients and roll the cookies out on cornmeal instead of a floured board.

Molasses Cookies

G et ready for twenty versions of molasses cookies. They were the kind of cookie Anna's grandmother would have made for her. In fact, I'll bet some of these enduring recipes did belong to her grandmother. They could even have been passed down by her great grandmother, as most of the following molasses/ginger cookie recipes changed little from the mid-19th century up to the time when Anna recorded them.

"N.O. molasses" referred to New Orleans molasses, a lighter and better tasting grade of molasses than the more refined, less expensive and bitter blackstrap molasses. When making these cookies, use the best molasses you can find. Home-grown is always best. Look for it in the Fall and grab a couple of quarts to keep on hand.

Molasses/Ginger Cookie Key:
Water, milk, cream, sour cream, coffee = cake-like texture
Boiled molasses – snappy, tough cookie (that's "good" tough)
Egg = tender if one is used, puffy if more
More than ½ cup molasses (and no other liquids) = a chewy cookie

Crunchy Gingerbread Folks
Use this recipe for the familiar gingerbread cookies of today as a reference when you're reading through Anna's molasses and ginger cookies. They're crunchy, spicy, buttery, and simple to make.

10 Tbs. unsalted butter	3 cups flour
½ cup packed brown sugar	¾ teaspoon soda
1 egg	¼ tsp. salt
½ cup molasses	2 tsp. ginger
1 tsp. cinnamon	¼ tsp. nutmeg
Pinch cloves or allspice	

Cream butter and sugar, then mix in egg and molasses. Sift together dry ingredients, and add to creamed mixture. Chill dough a few hours until you can handle it. Take out half at a time, roll ¼ inch thick and cut with floured cutters. Bake at 375° about 10 minutes or until lightly browned. These are the type you decorate with sprinkles, nuts, or raisins before baking or royal icing afterward.

Molasses Cookies

3. Molasses Cookies

Boil 5 minutes: 1 cup sugar, 1 cup molasses, 1 cup lard & butter, (mixed); set aside to cool. When cool add 2 well beaten eggs, 1 teaspoon cinnamon, 1 teaspoon ginger, and 1 teaspoon soda in ½ teacup of boiling water. Add flour to make a stiff dough.

Text (below) and Photo Courtesy of the Library of Congress

Rural Electrification in the U.S., 1940

"The electric range or stove in this American farm kitchen eliminates the need of building fires, carrying fuel and emptying ashes, thus allowing the housewife at least ten more hours per month for other tasks. If the range has an automatic timer, food can be placed in the oven long before it needs to start cooking; at the proper minute the heat will turn itself on and the cooking proceed at the proper length of time, then turn itself off again, all without attention."

MOLASSES COOKIES

4. MOLASSES COOKIES, MY OWN

1 egg, 1 teacup each of granulated sugar, & maple molasses, 1 tablespoon each of soda, & vinegar, & ½ tablespoon of ginger, ¼ teaspoon cloves. Flour enough to roll thin. Bake quickly. No shortning. Are nice.

Webster's 1913 dictionary defines maple molasses and maple honey as maple sap boiled to the consistency of molasses. Vinegar appears in the recipe because the acid found in molasses (needed for leavening along with baking soda) is lacking in maple syrup. This is a valiant attempt on Anna's part to make a tasty fat-free cookie. The word around here is that this cookie is better than a poke in the face, but barely. If you make them, omit the ginger because the combination of ginger and maple imparts an earthy flavor to the cookie, sort of like tree fungus or reindeer moss.

MAPLE MOLASSES ICE BOX COOKIES

Anna's maple molasses flavoring was just too wonderful an idea to let slide, so I boiled some maple syrup down by about a third until it matched the consistency of molasses and set out to create some really good maple cookies. The clear winner is Maple Brandy Snaps (see page 120), but this one is tasty as well. Walnuts go well with maple syrup, as does butter, so here's an old-timey recipe that makes use of both. My mom, Nancy Swell, calls these overnight cookies.

½ cup butter	½ tsp. cream of tartar
⅓ cup maple molasses	½ tsp. soda
½ cup brown sugar	Pinch salt
1 egg	1½ cups flour
1 tsp. vanilla	1 cup halved walnuts

Start with ½ cup real maple syrup and boil it down to ⅓ cup, then chill. Cream butter and sugar, add maple, egg, and vanilla. Sift dry ingredients and blend into creamed mixture. Stir in walnuts. Drop dough into a log shape on some waxed paper. Roll up and freeze until solid. Slice thin as you can, and bake on a greased cookie sheet in a 375° oven until light brown.

Note: You can substitute white sugar for the maple molasses and you'll get a nice, delicate, crispy, traditional cookie.

MOLASSES COOKIES

WILL COOKIES MAKE YOU FAT?

Fashion-dictated body proportions were undergoing a dramatic metamorphosis in the years between 1895 and 1920. From politics to petticoats, women of this era stood up for themselves as they grew weary of being squashed by corsets and society as well. They had suffered one bilious digestive misery too many. Ladies' fashions went from looking like the pinched outfit below in 1896 to a much more relaxed look in 1915.

As the corsets were tossed, there came an increased concern for slimming down and eating healthier foods. If corpulence was once a sign of 19th century prosperity, by 1910 it meant gluttony. Women weren't the only ones being targeted for weight loss in popular magazines; portly men were no longer attractive either.

Thus began the age of "The Dainty Dessert." Squirmy, but light, gelatin desserts sat gleaming on Mother Oats premium china dessert plates where once sat a big old slab of lemon pie. Oatmeal Fancies and Peanut Snaps

1896   *1915*

moved into lunch boxes where poundcake once resided. Cookies would only increase in popularity as the decades passed, until somehow, a hundred years later, they ended up as dinner-plate sized, artery clogging blobs of transfat and sugar. How did that happen? They started out as a light dessert. In answer to the question "Will cookies make you fat?", a few of Anna's won't; one modern giant deli cookie may!

DON'T STAY FAT
Obesity Quickly and Safely Cured.

ARE YOU **TOO FAT**

MOLASSES COOKIES

30. SPICE CAKE DROPS

1 cup each of butter, sugar, molasses & hot water, 5 cups flour, 3 eggs, 1 tablespoon soda, 1 teaspoon each of ginger, nutmeg, cinnamon & cloves.

34. CINNAMON DROPS

1 egg, 1 cup sugar, 1 cup molasses, ½ cup butter, 1 cup water, 2 teaspoons cinnamon, 1 heaping teaspoon soda, 5 cups flour.

36. WINE DROPS

1 cup each of butter, N.O. molasses, & sour milk, 2 cups sugar, 2 eggs, 1 teaspoonful each of soda, cinnamon, & cloves, 2 cups currants, or chopped raisins & 6 cups flour.

38. SPICE DROPS

½ cup sugar, ½ cup lard, 1 cup boiling water in which 2 teaspoons soda are dissolved; 1 cup molasses, 2½ cups flour, all kinds spices. This may be baked in muffin or cup cake tins, by omitting spices & baking in sheet, is delicious.

60. JUNGLE DROP COOKIES

1 cup sugar, ½ cup butter, ½ cup molasses, 1 egg, 1 cup buttermilk or coffee, 1 teaspoon soda, 1 teaspoon cinnamon, 1 tablespoon vanilla, pinch salt, flour enough to make a stiff batter. Drop from a spoon. Drop raisins, currants, or nuts on top if liked.

Molasses Cookies

71. Mamma Drop Cookies

1 cup brown sugar, 1½ cup molasses, ¾ cup butter, 2 eggs, 1 cup cream, 1 teaspoon ginger, 2 rounded teaspoons soda dissolved in sour cream or milk. Make batter stiff enough to drop on greased tins & bake.

97. Brown Cookies

3 teacups brown sugar, ½ lb. butter, 5 eggs, 1 pint molasses, 1 teacup milk, & 2 lbs. flour sifted with 3 teaspoons baking powder with ½ oz. cinnamon & a grated nutmeg. Drop the batter, allowing room to spread so cookies do not touch. Bake in quick oven.

The Fakir at Work

An interesting mid-19th century recipe. The addition of baking powder is odd in that soda is the leavening of choice for a molasses cookie. For a chewy, thin, robustly molasses-flavored cookie, try this version of Anna's brown cookies.

Chewy Molasses Cookies

½ cup butter	1 tsp. baking powder
1 cup brown sugar	½ tsp. soda
1 cup molasses	¼ tsp. salt
2 eggs	1 tsp. cinnamon
3 cups flour	½ tsp. nutmeg

Cream butter and sugar. Add eggs and molasses. Sift dry ingredients and add to wet. Refrigerate a couple of hours. Preheat oven to 375° and drop a test cookie on parchment paper or a greased cookie sheet. Flours vary so much that you may need to add up to ½ cup more if the cookie spreads too much or tastes too strong.

Molasses Cookies

200. Spice Drop Cookies

Yokes of 3 eggs, ½ cup butter, 1 cup molasses, ½ cup milk, 3 cups flour, 2 teaspoons baking powder, pinch salt, spice to taste. Drop on buttered paper tins & bake in hot oven.

119 & 161. Spice Drops

Yokes of 3 eggs, ½ cup butter, 1 cup molasses, ½ cup sweet milk, 3 cups flour, 3 teaspoons baking powder. Spice with ground nutmeg, cloves, cinnamon, & flavor with extract of lemon. Drop on tins lined with buttered paper. Bake quickly.

Same as no. 200, but a good illustration of what Anna means by "spice to taste." Spice drops must have been a favorite as they appear three times in her book.

134. Drop Molasses Cookies

2 cups molasses, 1 cup lard, ⅔ cup boiling water, 1 teaspoon soda, 1 tablespoon ginger, pinch of salt, flour enough to make a stiff batter. Drop by teaspoon on well greased pans & bake in a quick oven.

140. Molasses Cookies

3 eggs, 1 cup lard, ½ cup butter, 1 cup sugar, 1 cup molasses, 1 tablespoon cinnamon, 1 tablespoon ginger, 1 tablespoon salt. Mix soft, roll thick & bake.

186. Soft Molasses Cookies

⅔ cup molasses, ⅓ cup sugar, 1 teaspoon ginger, ½ teaspoon each of cinnamon & salt, 1 teaspoon soda dissolved in small ½ cup of warm milk or water, & ½ cup shortning melted. Mix in order given, flour enough to roll. Bake in hot oven, do not scorch or bake too long.

Molasses Cookies

109. Molasses Cookies

2 cups molasses, 1 cup butter, 2 eggs, 2 teaspoons soda, 2 teaspoons ginger, ½ teaspoon cloves, flour to mix soft. Roll thick, bake in moderate oven.

127. Plain Molasses Cookies

Mix: 1 cup molasses, ½ cup lard (melted), ½ cup (scant) of sour milk, pinch salt, 1 teaspoon soda, & flour enough to roll out in a sheet not too thick. Cut & bake in moderate oven. 1 heaping teaspoon ginger may be added.

188. Molasses Cookies

1 cup molasses, ½ cup brown sugar, 1 egg, ¾ cup lard or lard & butter mixed, ½ teaspoon each of cinnamon, & ginger, 1 teaspoon soda, & enough flour to roll thin. Bake in quick oven.

213. Roxbury Drops

Cream ½ cup sugar, ¼ cup butter, stir in ½ cup molasses & ½ cup sour milk. Add 1½ cups flour ½ teaspoon cloves, 1 teaspoon cinnamon & a little nutmeg. Beat the yolks of 2 eggs & add them. Then stir in ½ cup seedless raisins & ½ cup chopped nuts rolled in a little flour, a teaspoon soda dissolved in a little boiling water, & last the stiffly beaten whites of 2 eggs. The dough should be quite stiff. If necessary add a little more flour. Drop by teaspoon on buttered tin, leaving space between to spread & bake 15 to 20 minutes in a moderate oven.

GINGER COOKIES

You're probably wondering why most of the ginger cookies look just the same as the molasses cookies. I am too. Out of 21 different ginger cookie recipes, there are only two which don't call for molasses. My expert opinion based on eating way too many gingerbread cookies is that molasses cookies and ginger cookies are the same thing. The rolled or dropped ginger cookies are cake-like, very old-fashioned, and not that sweet. Gingersnaps are made without milk, cream, or water and are thin, crunchy and spicy.

10. GINGER COOKIES EGGLESS

Cream ½ cup butter, 1 cup brown sugar. Add ½ cup milk, mix & add 2 cups flour; with 2 teaspoons baking powder, 1½ teaspoon ginger. Mix all well & drop by teaspoon on well greased pan. Bake in moderate hot oven 20 minutes.

50. BOHEMIAN GINGER COOKIES

1½ lbs. flour, 1 lb. powdered sugar, 1 teacup honey, 4 eggs, 4 tablespoons sour cream, 1 tablespoon soda, 1 teaspoon cloves, 1 teaspoon cinnamon, 1 teaspoon of vanilla, ½ cup chopped & candied orange peal. (First put soda in sour cream.) Mix all well together. Roll out quite thin, cut shapes desired. Press an almond in center (first split in half), bake. These are hard at first when baked but soften in jar.

SURPRISE!!!!! There's no ginger in this ginger cookie recipe. A far-out Bohemian cookie, indeed. Really, I'll bet a teaspoon of ginger should be substituted for the cloves.

A Little Ironing Suggestion
Modern Priscilla, Jan. 1915
When the top of the stove is full and it is time to get dinner with still some ironing to be accomplished, the irons can be heated very nicely in the oven.

GINGER COOKIES

GINGER SNAPS

And if to make the best you'd wish to know,
Why, study well the lines you find below;
Melt of butter half a pound; also of lard;
Then add sugar brown a half a pound.
Stir in a quart of 'lasses, not too hard,
Four tablespoons of ginger nicely ground.
Into this mixture sift two quarts of flour,
Then, to insure the cake shall not be sour,
Dissolve in milk four teaspoonsfuls of soda;
(Saleratus is advised, but I like not the odor).
Mix either with milk; it surely makes no matter,
So that you pour the milk into the batter.
Add more flour and roll out thin the dough;
Then cut in cakes, but this you surely know.
Bake them well in an oven cooks call "slow."
And when they are baked they will not last long, I know.

Sister Alice Funderburg, Gillford, Mo.
Inglenook Cook Book, 1911

5. GINGER COOKIES

Mix 1 cup molasses, ½ cup sugar, & a cup shortning: add 2½ cups flour: with 2 teaspoons soda, 1 tablespoon ginger, ½ teaspoon cloves, cinnamon & salt. Mix well with 1 cup of boiling hot water, add quickly 2 well beaten eggs. It looks thin but don't add any more flour. Drop by teaspoon on well greased tin, well apart. When done let cool in same tin, as they break easily. When cool frost with white frosting. These keep moist for 2 weeks.

GINGER COOKIES

6. SOUR MILK GINGER COOKIES

Mix ¼ cup lard, 1 cup sugar, 1 egg, add ½ cup molasses, 2 teaspoons ginger, 1 of cinnamon, ½ teaspoon soda, ½ teaspoon salt. Add 1¾ cups flour. Drop on waxed sheet & bake in moderate hot oven.

32. GINGER DROPS

2 cups molasses, 1 cup lard, ½ cup milk, 1 tablespoonful each of ginger & soda, 2 eggs, add enough flour to mix as soft as possible & drop.

43. GINGER DROP CAKES

3 eggs, 1 cup lard, 1 cup molasses, 1 cup brown sugar, 1 tablespoon ginger, 1 tablespoon soda (dissolved in a cup of boiling water), 5 cups flour. Mix & drop well apart on greased pan.

47. GINGER COOKIES

1 cup of N.O. molasses, 1 cup brown sugar, 2 cups thick sour cream, 1 big cup butter, 2 eggs, 3 tablespoons soda, 2 tablespoons of ginger, & flour to make a soft dough. Roll out very thin; cut & bake in a quick oven.

Author's Note: This is WAY too much soda. 2 tsp. is plenty. One tsp. per cup of molasses, or ½ tsp. per cup of flour should be enough for most of the cookies in this chapter.

57. FAY GINGER COOKIES

½ cup sugar, ½ cup lard, 1 cup molasses, 1½ cups flour, 1 cup boiling water, 2 teaspoons soda dissolved in boiling water. 1 teaspoon each of ginger & cinnamon. Beat 2 eggs well & put them in last. Drop from teaspoon into baking pan about 2 inches apart. Bake in hot oven.

GINGER COOKIES

67. GINGER SNAPS

1 cup sugar, 1 cup sorghum, 1 cup lard, 1 tablespoon (scant) ginger, 1 teaspoon salt, 1 teaspoon black pepper, 1 tablespoon soda dissolved in ⅔ cup of boiling water. Flour enough to roll. Roll thin & bake in hot oven.

Speaking of adding pepper to ginger cookies, I thought I'd compare some late-19th century European biscuit recipes to the cookies Americans were eating about the same time to see if there was much difference. That's how I found this really interesting recipe for zippy "Laugh-

ing or Fun Nuts." It's from *The Bread & Biscuit Bakers and Sugar Boiler's Assistant* by Robert Wells published in London in 1890. The fun part comes with the burn that follows after the cookie is eaten. While our tasters weren't wild about them, cayenne is found in the store-bought variety you grew up on. Add a little dash of hot fun to your ginger snaps and see what you think.

LAUGHING OR FUN NUTS

"1 lb. of gingerbread dough, 3 ozs. of butter, 3 ozs. of sugar, 1 oz. of cayenne pepper. Mix all together, pin out in a sheet, one-eighth of an inch thick. Cut them out the size of a penny. They are very hot."

If you will rub your new tin ware with lard and heat it thoroughly in the oven, it will never rust.
Dr. Miles Nervine, 1920

GINGER COOKIES

68. GINGER SNAPS

1 cup lard, 1 cup molasses, 1 cup brown sugar, boil together. Add while hot 2 cups flour. Dissolve 3 teaspoons soda in 1 tablespoon vinegar & add when cool. Then stir in 1 egg, & 1 tablespoon each of ginger & cinnamon & ½ teaspoon cloves. Add ¼ cup corn starch & enough flour to make a stiff dough. Roll very thin & bake in a brisk oven.

LITTLE CRACKLE-TOP GINGER SNAPS

Here's a contemporary recipe for ginger snaps that's similar to number 68, but you'll find them a bit more tender, and crackly-topped too.

¾ cup butter	3½ cup flour
¾ cup brown sugar	1 tsp. baking soda
¾ cup white sugar	3 tsp. ginger
2 eggs	1 tsp. cinnamon
½ cup molasses	½ tsp. salt
2 tsp. vinegar	

Cream butter and sugar. Beat in eggs, molasses, and vinegar. Sift dry ingredients and blend well. Roll or scoop dough into 1 inch balls and brush lightly with water. Bake on greased cookie sheet or parchment paper about 12 minutes until medium brown at 325º.

79. GINGER COOKIES WITH ICING

1 cup sugar, ½ cup butter, ½ cup lard, 1 cup sorghum, 2 eggs, 1 tablespoon ginger, 1 level teaspoon soda dissolved in ½ teacup of warm water, 2 teaspoons cinnamon, ½ teaspoon cloves (scant) & flour to roll. Cut and bake, and when cool frost.

80. WHITE BOILED ICING FOR COOKIES

1 cup sugar, ½ cup boiling water, boil until it threads from spoon & then add gradually to well beaten whites of 2 eggs, beating until cold. Flavor to taste.

GINGER COOKIES

115. GINGER SNAPS

1¼ cups flour, ¼ cup sugar, 2 tablespoons butter, ½ pint molasses, 2 teaspoons baking powder, 3 tablespoons extract of Jamaica ginger.

D 138 **Essence of Jamaica Ginger.** This is a strong essence prepared from selected Jamaica Ginger Root, it contains all the stimulating warming and healing properties of good ginger and will be found very valuable in stomach and bowel troubles.

This size usually sold poor in quality at 25c. Our price full strength 18c. Regular 50c size; our price, 36c.

~1896 Sears & Roebuck Catalog

The Ginger Jake Blues

The 1896 Sears and Roebuck catalog offered Jamaica Ginger both as a flavoring extract in 2 oz. bottles as well as a "tonic" in 4 oz. bottles, that promised to deliver both pep and digestive health in addition to ginger flavor. However, most of the pep came from the product's 70% alcohol content. No wonder Jamaican Ginger extract was a favorite beverage flavoring during the prohibition era.

The Ginger Jake sold up until 1930 was fine, but in January of 1930, one of the manufacturers of the product added an adulterant called TOCP to the tonic. The Jake buzz came at a great cost when fifty thousand Ginger Jake users suffered varying degrees of often irreversible paralysis due to the neurotoxic effects of TOCP. Victims developed a characteristic high-stepping, foot flopping gait commonly known as the "Jake Walk," which became the inspiration for a number of popular songs at the time.

GINGER COOKIES

The Jake Walk Blues
Recorded by The Allen Brothers in 1930

I can't eat, I can't talk
Been drinkin' mean jake, Lord, now can't walk
Ain't got nothin' now to lose
Cause I'm a jake walkin' papa with the jake walk blues.

Listen here papa, can't you see
You can't drink jake, and get along with me
You're a jake walkin' papa with the jake walk blues
I'm a red hot mama that you can't afford to lose.

Listen here daddy, while I tell you once more
If you're gonna drink jake don't you knock at my door
Listen here mama have to call your hand
I'm a jake walkin' papa from jake walk land.

I'm not good lookin' and I'm not low down
I'm a jake walkin' papa just hangin' around
Now I've made this song and it may not rhyme
But I'm a jake walkin' papa just havin' a good time.

My daddy was a gambler and a drunkard too
If he was living today he'd have the jake walk too
When I die you can have my hand
Gonna take a bottle of jake to the promised land.

Spoken:
Now I'm feelin' kinda drunk, brother
Be a wearin' jake socks after awhile
You know they call them iron socks
You know, I bet you don't know
       one from the other, brother, which is the other?

GINGER COOKIES

92. GINGER SNAPS

Boil 2 cups molasses for 3 minutes & add to it, 1 cup butter, 1 teaspoon baking powder with sufficient flour to work into smooth batter, & add 1 tablespoon ginger. Work as soft as possible, the softer the better to roll. Cut & bake. Or use only enough flour to make a stiff batter to drop from spoon. Then drop & bake.

These tough cookies will yank your two front teeth right out of your head as written. However, boiling the molasses gives the cookies a snappy and chewy texture and a shiny surface. Try this version with an egg added for just a little tenderness:

½ cup molasses	1 tsp. soda
6 tbs. butter	Pinch salt
1 egg	2 cups flour
½ cup brown sugar	1 tsp. each ginger and cinnamon

Boil molasses 2 minutes, then add butter. When cool, add brown sugar and beaten egg. Sift dry ingredients together, stir into wet mixture. Drop by spoonfuls onto parchment paper or a buttered baking sheet. Bake 10 minutes at 350°. After they bake about 5 minutes, quickly sprinkle raw sugar on top, then return to oven to finish baking.

GINGER COOKIES

Molasses Making in Virginia, 1938

123. GINGER SNAPS

Mix ½ cup granulated sugar, 1 cup molasses, ½ cup lard, ¼ cup lukewarm water in which dissolve 1 teaspoon soda, ½ teaspoon salt, 1 teaspoon cinnamon, 1 heaping teaspoon ginger, 4 cups flour. Mix all together & work well. This dough should be rather stiff. Let it stand covered with a damp towel, as long as possible. If convenient, over night. Kneed it well until very smooth. Roll out thin & cut out with small cutter. Put in pan & cover tops with damp towel just before baking, which makes them crack nicely. Oven should not be very hot.

A nice crinkle-top, crunchy gingersnap. For a spicier cookie, try this version of Anna's recipe no. 123.

¼ cup sugar	Pinch salt
½ cup molasses	½ tsp. soda dissolved in a tsp. water
6 tbs. butter	¾ tsp. ginger
¾ cup flour	½ tsp. cinnamon

Mix as above and cover overnight with a damp towel. Next day, chill the dough just a bit. Knead, adding up to ¼ cup more flour, and roll out thin. Brush cookies lightly with water before baking in a 350° oven for about 10 minutes.

GINGER COOKIES

T he only thing missing in Anna's gingerbread cookie recipes is a bit of fresh orange peel. The recipe below for Orange Gingerbread cookies is basically the same as Anna's no. 123 except for the addition of 3 oz. of fresh orange zest. These cookies, from an 1831 cookbook called *The Cook Not Mad,* would have been cut into card shapes before being decorated with a checker pattern.

No. 130.   *Orange Gingerbread*

"Two pounds and a quarter fine flour, a pound and 3 quarters molasses, 12 ounces of sugar, 2 ounces undried orange peel chopped fine, 1 ounce each of ginger and allspice, melt twelve ounces of butter, mix the whole together, lay it by for twelve hours, roll it out with as little flour as possible, cut in pieces three inches wide, mark them in the form of checkers with the back of a knife, rub them over with the yelk of an egg, beat with a tea cup of milk, when done wash them again with the egg."

with the

BOSS
ALWAYS ⟶ REGISTERED U.S. PATENT OFFICE ⟶ AHEAD

GLASS DOOR OVEN

117. GINGER COOKIES

2 cups molasses, 1 cup lard, 1 cup sugar, ½ cup sour cream, 1 tablespoon ginger, 2 eggs, 3 ½ teaspoons soda, flour to roll thick. Bake in quick oven.

GINGER COOKIES

118. GINGER DROPS

1 cup molasses, ½ cup brown sugar, ½ cup butter, 1 teaspoon each of extract of ginger & cinnamon, 2 teaspoon soda in 1 cup of hot water, 3 cups flour, 2 eggs. Bake in drops in buttered tins.

131. GINGER DROPS COOKIES

½ cup sugar, 1 cup molasses, ½ cup butter, 1 teaspoon cinnamon, ginger & cloves, 2 level teaspoons soda in 1 cup boiling water, 2½ cups flour. Add 2 well beaten eggs last thing before baking. Drop from spoon & bake.

136. GINGER COOKIES

2 cups molasses, 1 cup melted lard, 1 cup sugar, ½ cup sour cream (fill up with sweet milk), 2 teaspoons ginger, 1 teaspoon cinnamon, 3 teaspoons soda stirred in the flour & 1 teaspoon soda in the milk, 2 eggs.

137. GINGER COOKIES

1½ cups molasses, ½ cup brown sugar, ¼ cup lard, 1 cup sour cream (or milk), 1 tablespoon ginger, 1 tablespoon cinnamon, ½ teaspoon cloves, 1 tablespoon soda, pinch salt. Flour enough to roll out. Cut & bake in quick oven. This makes about 100 2-inch cookies.

138. GINGER SNAPS

1 cup molasses, ½ cup brown sugar, 1 teaspoon ginger, 1 teaspoon melted lard. Add flour and mix not too stiff. Roll & cut in shapes.

139. GINGER SNAPS

1 cup brown sugar, 1 cup molasses, 1 cup lard, 1 teaspoon soda, ¾ cup water, 1 teaspoon ginger, ½ teaspoon cinnamon. Mix well & add flour enough to roll out. Cut & bake.

FILLED COOKIES

Photo by Walker Evans, 1938   *Courtesy of the Library of Congress*

FILLED COOKIES

Filled cookies are an adventure to make as well as an adventure to eat. They really do seem to be everybody's favorite cookie. Not unlike pie, filled cookies are mysterious, often wholesome, and special because they're a bit of trouble to make. Once you find a good recipe that works for you, you can fill the cookies with just about any dried fruit, nut, or jam combination you can imagine.

1. FILLED COOKIES

2 cups rolled oats, 3 cups flour, 1 teaspoon salt, 2 cups sugar, 1 cup shortning, 1 cup sour milk with 1 teaspoon soda dissolved in the milk. Cream the sugar & shortning, mix flour, oat meal, & salt & add milk. Mix stiff & roll very thin. Cut with cookie cutter & on each one put a teaspoon of prunes & raisins cooked together. Cover with another cookie & press edges together.

See pages 98 and 99 for a detailed description of how to make these unbelievably fabulous cookies.

26. FIG COOKIES

1 cup sugar, 1 egg, ½ cup melted butter, ½ cup sour milk with 1 teaspoon soda. Flavor to taste, roll very thin. Place a spoonful of filling on center of cookie, place another cookie on top & press lightly around down edge.

Note: Add enough flour to roll very thin. For filling recipe, see page 74.

To clean kitchen tables, pastry boards and rolling pins, cut a lemon in half and rub it over the entire surface of the wood. Then rinse with clear water.

When a glass stopper sticks, tap it gently with another piece of glass.

~Dr. Miles Nervine, 1920

FILLED COOKIES

8. FIG BARS

Use any choice receipt for cookies; roll the dough thin & cut in long narrow cakes (a mustard-box with hole punched in the bottom makes a good cutter). Grease baking pan, fill it with the cakes, not too close together, spread each not quite to the edge with cooked fig paste, brush the edge with cold water, & place another cake on top, pressing the edges together, brush over with beaten white of an egg, dredge with gra. sugar, & bake about 10 minutes. Lift from tin with cake-turner. White of egg & sugar may be omitted, the bars baked as plain cookies.

Note: For recipe and filling, see page 74.

Strategy

Not having a mustard box from 1917, I improvised by popping the plastic lid off a 5-oz. tin of Hungarian paprika only to find a tidy rolled edge at the end of the can. Now you can't cut cookie dough with that, so I grabbed my pliers and straightened out the rolled edge to form the perfect cutter for an old timey "Fig Newton" cookie. You can always make these cookies up by an easier means, but I just had to find out for myself how they would turn out as written. Another method that's even older is to divide the dough in half and roll out each half into equal-sized rectangles using lightly floured waxed paper. Drop dots of filling over all as though you were making ravioli. Lightly brush the edges around filling with water. Now place the other layer of dough on top. Press down to seal around filling and cut with a pie jagger (a crimped edge pastry wheel). Use a cake-turner to lift onto parchment-lined cookie sheet. After trying both these techniques, I now know why commercially produced fig newtons became popular in the 1910's.

The third method I attempted after running out of patience with the first two was what I call "the ditch method." Rolling the dough into a long snake, I took the handle of a wooden spoon and made a ditch all along the dough. After cramming the filling down in the dough, I pinched the dough around it and sliced off cookies, Newton style. As you can see by the handy chart on the next page, there are advantages and disadvantages to each strategy.

FILLED COOKIES

Here's a brief critique of all three methods:

Paprika can: *Pretty shape, good distribution of filling, a pain to make.*
Ravioli: *Ugly, big portion of filling in one spot, a bit tricky to make, but quicker than the paprika can method.*
Ditch: *Fair to look at, big with not enough filling and very easy to make.*

Method 1: Paprika can

Method 2: Ravioli style

Method 3: The ditch

Photos by Wes Erbsen

The Final Analysis

Wouldn't you know, Anna wins, according to our numerous taste testers. My recommendation is to use whatever method you like and if you go to these lengths to analyze the winning technique, you have too much time on your hands!

FILLED COOKIES

66. FILLED COOKIES

1 cup sugar, ½ cup lard, ½ cup milk, 1 egg, 2 heaping teaspoons baking powder, 2 cups flour, pinch salt.

Fill with filling:
1 cup sugar, 1 cup raisins or figs, ½ cup chopped nuts, 1 teaspoon lemon, 1 tablespoon flour, ½ cup hot water. Boil until smooth. Roll out cookies & put into pan. Put a spoonful of filling on each cookie. Put another cookie on top. Pinch around to hold together & bake.

You'll need 3 cups of flour, not 2, to make these Anna's way. Adding a little buttermilk gives them a slightly cake-like consistency. If you substitute buttermilk, you need to use soda instead of baking powder for leavening. Since the fruit filling is so strong, I like the cookie less sweet, so I only use ¾ cup sugar instead of 1 cup.

1 cup sugar	2 cups flour
½ cup butter	pinch salt
1 egg	1 tsp. soda
¼ cup buttermilk	1 tsp. vanilla

Cream butter and sugar, then beat in egg and vanilla. Add soda to buttermilk and blend in. Mix the salt with the flour, then combine mixture and refrigerate at least 2 hours until firm.

FIG FILLING

1 cup chopped, dried organic figs
½ cup coarsely ground walnuts
Juice of ¼ lemon
¼ cup brown sugar
¼ cup white sugar
½ cup water

Cook figs in water until softened. Add sugars and cook another minute. Give it a few whirls in the food processor until mostly smooth. Stir in lemon juice and walnuts and refrigerate along with the cookie dough.

FILLED COOKIES

RUM RAISIN PEEK-A-BOO COOKIES

From a Salem, West Virginia, 1970's church cookbook comes this great recipe. It's almost identical to Anna's Filled Cookies no. 66, but the cookies are very quick and simple to make. AND, they are just terrific! The raisins will bubble out of the top of the cookie a bit.

1 cup shortening (butter)　3 cups flour
2 cups brown sugar　　　　1 tsp. soda
2 eggs　　　　　　　　　　½ tsp. salt
1 tsp. vanilla

Cream butter and sugar until fluffy, beat in eggs and vanilla. Add flour sifted with soda and salt and beat until combined. Drop a spoonful onto greased cookie sheet 2 inches apart. Press a scant tsp. of filling down into each mound and cover filling with a little more dough. Bake at 350° about 12 minutes until light brown and bubbly.

Filling:

1½ cup raisins　　　　½ cup water
⅓ cup sugar　　　　　1 Tbs. lemon juice
1 Tbs. corn starch　　1 Tbs. butter
¼ cup chopped nuts　3 Tbs. rum (author's addition)

Dissolve cornstarch in the water. Simmer raisins and sugar in the water until mixture thickens, about 5 minutes. Don't let it burn. Add butter, nuts, rum, then cool to room temperature.

213. FILLED COOKIES

1 cup butter, 2 cups sugar, 1 cup sour cream, 3 eggs, 1 teaspoon soda & flavor to suit. Mix soft, roll thin, cut, put in pan, place a spoonful of filling on each cooky. Lay another cooky on top & bake in quick oven.

Filling: 1 cup raisins chopped, ¾ cup sugar, 1 cup boiling water, & a tablespoon flour stirred in little cold water. Cook until the mixture thickens.

FRUIT COOKIES

T his group of cookies smells like Christmas. The combination of cinnamon, nutmeg, cloves, allspice and chopped fruits and nuts found in most of the following recipes will fill your home with holiday aromas all year long. Hermits are spiced cookies sometimes containing fruit that are either rolled or dropped. Rocks contain similar spices but are loaded with dried fruit and nuts and are dropped in a bumpy pile and baked. The innards of Anna's hermits, rocks, and fruit cookies are sort of all the same with the usual variations in butter, sugar, eggs, and flour. She does include a couple of her own interesting original recipes. Our favorite is no. 73, the Not-Baked Fruit Cookies. You'll think you're doing something good for your body as you scarf these dried fruit and nut morsels which I recommend you douse liberally with rum.

Courtesy of Library of Congress

"Their first glimpse." Photo by D.J. Burrell, 1908

FRUIT COOKIES

11. GOOD DROP COOKIES

2 cups brown sugar, ¾ cup butter, 2 beaten eggs, 2 teaspoons soda dissolved in ½ cup hot water, 3 cups flour, & 1 cup each of chopped raisins & currants. Drop by small spoonfuls on well greased pan & bake in moderate hot oven.

12. BOSTON COOKIES

1 cup butter, 1½ cup sugar, 3 eggs, 1 teaspoon soda, 1 ½ teaspoon hot water, 3¼ cups flour, pinch salt, 1 teaspoon cinnamon, 1 cup chopped nutmeats, ½ cup raisins, ½ cup currants, all chopped. Cream butter with sugar, add eggs, then flour with soda & spices then nuts raisins & etc. Drop & bake in moderately hot oven. These will keep good, the older they are the better.

22. FRUIT COOKIES #1

1 cup butter, 2 cups sugar, 3 eggs, 1 teaspoon soda dissolved in ½ cup boiling water, 1 teaspoon each of cinnamon, cloves, & nutmeg, 1 cup each of (chopped) raisins & currants, & flour enough to make a stiff batter. Drop from a teaspoon on a greased pan 3 in. apart as they spread. Nuts may be added.

25. HERMITS

Beat 1 egg to a froth with 1½ cup sugar, add 1 cup sour milk (cream is best), & 1 cup flour, with which sift 1 teaspoon each of soda, & cinnamon; & ½ teaspoon each of cloves, allspice, & nutmeg, pinch of salt, 1 cup chopped raisins, & enough more flour to make a dough to roll out. Cut with cookie cutter & bake in a moderate oven.

FRUIT COOKIES

33. BOSTON FRUIT COOKIES #2

1 cup butter, 1½ cups sugar, 3 cups flour, 1 cup chopped raisins, 3 eggs, 1½ teaspoons soda in a little hot water, 1 ½ teaspoons cinnamon, 1 teaspoon cloves, 1 of nutmeg, pinch of salt. Drop on floured sheets.

Same as fruit cookies no. 1, only ½ cup less sugar and no water.

35. APPLE SAUCE DROP COOKIES

1 cup hot apple sauce with 1 teaspoon of soda beaten well through it, ½ cup butter, 1½ cups sugar, 1 cup raisins, spice to suit, & add flour until it will not spread when piled.

You would never believe that this recipe would work without egg, but these cake-like spicy cookies are quite good. Try with half unpacked brown sugar, half white, ¼ tsp. salt, 1 tsp. cinnamon, 1 teaspoon ginger, 2 cups flour and ½ cup walnuts. Bake at 360° about 12-15 minutes. Makes about 4½ dozen. Kids can taste this raw eggless batter, but you might want to leave the raisins and nuts out of their baked cookies.

44. FRUIT COOKIES # 3

1½ cups sugar, 2 eggs, ¼ cup sweet milk, 1 teaspoon soda, ½ teaspoon cream of tartar, 1 teaspoon each of cloves, mace, nutmeg, & cinnamon, & 1 cup currants or raisins. Flour enough to roll out, & bake.

52. RAISIN HERMITS

1½ cups brown sugar, ⅔ cup butter, 1 cup seeded raisins, 1 teaspoon each of soda, cinnamon, & cloves, 3 cups flour. Mix well & drop by tablespoon well apart.

Recipe is missing eggs, or other liquid. You can try with 2 eggs.

FRUIT COOKIES

Raisins: Seeded or Seedless?

Some of the older recipes here will request that you seed your raisins, and others call for seedless varieties. Prior to 1876, bakers had to seed their own domestic raisins with a raisin seeder or deal with messy stuck together raisins that were pre-seeded. According to *The Grocer's Encyclopedia* of 1911, grocers at that time stocked domestic seedless Thompsons, seeded and unseeded Muscats, imported naturally seedless Sultanas, and seeded Valencias on stalk and in seeded loose form. By 1917, cookie bakers didn't need to do much raisin seeding at home, and that's why most of Anna's recipes just call for "raisins."

58. HAZEL COOKIES

Cream 1 cup butter, 2 cups sugar, add 3 eggs well beaten. 1 teaspoon soda, 1 teaspoon cinnamon, ½ teaspoon cloves, 1 cup flour, 1 teaspoon baking powder. Sift dry ingredients & add enough flour to roll. Put in any fruit desired, raisins, figs, dates, & old fashioned walnuts.

70. ARMONA FRUIT COOKIES

2 cups sugar, ½ cup butter, 2 cups raisins, 2 eggs, ½ cup sour milk, 2 tablespoons cinnamon, 1 teaspoon cloves, 1 teaspoon nutmegs, ½ cup molasses, 1 teaspoon soda. Flour enough to roll out. Cut & bake.

72. RHUBARB COOKIES

"Made up by me." - Anna

1 cup stewed rhubarb, 1 cup shortening, 1 cup sugar, 1 teaspoon cinnamon, ½ teaspoon cloves, dash of nutmeg, ½ teaspoon soda dissolved in rhubarb, 2 cups flour, 2 teaspoons baking powder (scant). 1 cup raisins, 1 cup currants, & ½ cup chopped nuts. Drop from spoon.

FRUIT COOKIES

73. NOT BAKED FRUIT COOKIES
"Made up by me." - Anna

½ lb. dates chopped fine; ½ lb. figs; ½ lb. citron, ½ lb. seedless raisins; ½ lb. walnut meat, ½ lb. almonds. Grind all together fine, then roll in a cup of powdered sugar. Roll up like a long roll & slice off cookies the desired thickness. Wrap each cookie in wax paper. Keep in a cool place. Are very nice and will keep a long time. Do not bake them.

WOW!!!!! Anna is good. You can whip up a batch of these healthy, wholesome, and naturally sweet treats in a jiffy. I'd make a small batch first to see if you like them, because dried fruit and nuts are pricey. Place ½ cup each of dates, figs, raisins, walnuts, and almonds in a food processor fitted with a steel blade. Many folks have an aversion to citron, so a good substitute is candied orange peel, but only add about ¼ cup. Grind the mixture well, and add 2 tablespoons of rum, brandy, or good whiskey. Give the mixture another whirl, then roll into a log. Coat the log with confectioner's sugar; you'll have to rub it on to get it to stick. Cut into ½ inch pieces with a real sharp knife and layer on sheets of waxed paper in an airtight tin. These will only improve with age if they don't get gobbled up first.

Cherry-Apricot-Coconut Fruit Cookies

Combine equal parts dried apricots, dried tart cherries, white raisins, with the same amount of either almonds, pecans, or walnuts. Process until fine and stir in as much coconut as you like. Moisten with dark rum or Grand Marnier (orange liqueur), and roll in powdered sugar and slice. OR you can omit the coconut from the mixture and roll the log in the coconut instead of powdered sugar before slicing.

THE CHERRY SEEDER

FRUIT COOKIES

75. FRUIT COOKIES

1½ cups sugar, 2 eggs, 5 tablespoons sweet milk, 1 teaspoon soda, 1 teaspoon each of cloves, mace, nutmeg & cinnamon & 1 cup currants or raisins. ½ cup shortening, flour enough to roll out & bake.

78. FRUIT COOKIES

1½ cups brown sugar, 1 cup butter, 3 eggs, 5 table-spoons hot water, 1 teaspoon soda, 1 teaspoon cinnamon, ½ teaspoon cloves, ½ cup currants, ½ cup raisins, 1 cup chopped English walnuts & 3 cups flour.

98. DROP COOKIES

1 cup butter, ½ cup sugar, 2 eggs, 1 teaspoon baking powder, 1 pt. flour, 1 cup currants, 1 teaspoon each of extract of nutmeg & lemon, ½ cup milk. Mix into a rather firm batter & drop with a spoon on greased tin & bake in a quick oven 10 minutes.

108. FRUIT COOKIES

2 cups sugar, 1 cup butter, 2 cups chopped raisins, 2 eggs, 2 tablespoons sour milk, 1 teaspoon soda, ½ teaspoon each of extract nutmeg & cinnamon, flour enough to roll. Bake in quick oven.

Fruit Cookies

124. Rock Cookies

Mix well 1½ cups brown sugar, 1 cup butter or lard, pinch salt, 1 teaspoon cinnamon, 2 eggs, 3 tablespoons sour cream (or milk or buttermilk) with 1 teaspoon soda. Add 2 cups flour, ½ cup raisins, ½ cup currants (sprinkled with flour). Mix all well together; roll out & cut. Mark each cookie crosswise with a fork & bake.

130. Fruit Bars-Cookies

1 lb. sugar, 6 oz. lard, 2 eggs, ½ cup lukewarm water in which dissolve 1 teaspoon soda, ½ cup molasses, ¼ teaspoon cinnamon, ¼ teaspoon nutmeg, ¼ teaspoon allspice, pinch salt, ¾ lb. currants, ¾ lb. raisins, 1½ lbs. flour. Mix & roll out. Cut with long cutter, empty spice can will do. Lay in greased tin, brush over with egg & milk mixed, sprinkle over with choped nuts & bake.

133. Currant Cookies

2 eggs, 1½ cup sugar, 1 cup shortning, 1 cup sweet milk, 1 cup currants, a little candied citron, 1 teaspoon cinnamon, ¼ teaspoon nutmeg, & flour enough to roll out (mixed with) 2 heaping teaspoons baking powder. Mix soft. These will keep a long time. Cut small cookies & bake in quick oven.

135. Fruit Cookies

1 cup butter, 1 cup sugar, 3 eggs, ½ cup molasses, 1 teaspoon soda, 1 cup each of raisins, currants, & choped nuts, 1 teaspoon each of ginger, cloves, cinnamon & allspice, pinch salt. Flour to roll as soft as can be cut.

FRUIT COOKIES

151. HERMITS

1 cup butter, 1 cup sugar, 3 eggs, 1 teaspoon each of cloves, cinnamon & nutmeg, ½ teaspoon soda, 1 cup chopped raisins, 1 cup currants, ½ cup citron. Mix with enough flour to roll well, cut & bake in quick oven.

160. HERMITS HOBBY LIKES

3 eggs, 1 cup butter, 1½ cup sugar, 1 cup seeded & chopped raisins, a very little citron choped fine, 4 table-spoons whiskey, 1 teaspoon each of cloves, allspice & cinnamon, flour enough to roll them. Cut in rounds. These are very nice & will keep like a fruit cake. This is a guess work by Mrs. J. E. Suchanek. Are also named "hermits Hobby likes" as your papa always likes these.

This is a spicy cake-like version of hermits that became popular in the 1920's and 1930's despite prohibition's clamp-down on whiskey. Brandy or orange flavored liquor can be substituted for the whiskey. You can soak whole raisins in enough whiskey or brandy to cover before adding them to the dough. Just for fun, I used dried cherries, instead, which didn't go great with the spices, but made for an interesting cookie anyway. Use ¾ cup brown sugar, ¾ cup white sugar, about 2 to 2½ cup flour, and add 1 cup chopped walnuts and ¼ tsp. salt. Hobby must have been a big clove fan; I'd cut the cloves and allspice at least by half. Drop by spoonful onto parchment paper and bake 10 minutes or so at about 350°. You can also form into logs, freeze, slice and bake about 10 minutes until light brown.

194. DROP CAKES COOKIES

1 cup butter, ½ cup sugar, 2 eggs, 1 teaspoon baking powder, 1 pint flour, 1 cup currants, 1 teaspoon each of extract nutmeg & lemon, ½ cup milk. "Rub the butter & sugar to white light cream," add the eggs, beat 10 minutes, add flour & baking powder sifted together, the milk & extracts. Mix into a rather firm batter & drop with a spoon on a greased baking tin. Bake in quick oven.

FRUIT COOKIES

199. EDENKOBERS

2 eggs, 1 cup sugar, ¼ lb. almonds, pounded to paste, ¼ lb. chopped citron, ¼ lb. chopped candied lemon peel, 2 tablespoons drained honey, 2 cups flour, ½ teaspoon baking powder. Mix to a paste, roll out & cut in small cookies. Bake in moderate oven.

Edenkobers appeared in the 1902 (see right) and later versions of the *Royal Baking Powder Baker and Pastry Cook*. The interesting recipe is similar to German Pferffernusse (Peppernuts) and Danish Pebernoddder, without the cinnamon, cardamom, and other warm spices. The cookies also closely resemble Lebkuchen, of German origin as well, which are baked in a shallow tin, then cut into squares and frosted.

PEPPER-KOBERS

A combination of Edenkobers and Peppernuts, how can you resist these little fruity, spicy, cognac-glazed bites?

½ cup unsalted butter	½ cup ground almonds
1 cup packed brown sugar	1 tsp. cinnamon
3 Tbs. honey	½ tsp. ginger
1 egg	1 tsp. cardamom
2¼ cup flour	¼ tsp. pepper
1 tsp. baking powder	¼ cup chopped citron
½ tsp. salt	¼ cup candied lemon peel

Cream butter, sugar, and honey. Add egg. Sift dry ingredients and add to creamed mixture. Stir in citron and peel. Form dough into long, skinny, 1-inch wide snakes, wrap in plastic wrap and chill overnight. To bake, slice off ½ inch pieces and bake on greased tin about 8 minutes at 375°. While still warm, brush cognac glaze over the top. Store cooled cookies in an airtight tin between layers of waxed paper.

Cognac Glaze: Stir together ½ cup powdered sugar with a tablespoon more or less of cognac. Stir until a smooth consistency you can brush onto tops of cookies.

FRUIT COOKIES

Mighty dressed up for churning in 1902.

CHERRY STONER

221. PRUNE COOKIES

1 cup sugar, 1 cup shortning, 1 cup prunes (chopped fine), ¼ cup milk, 3 teaspoons baking powder, ½ teaspoon cinnamon, pinch salt, & 4 cups flour or enough to roll. Cream sugar, shortning & prunes together. Add milk, cinnamon, salt & baking powder with 3 cups flour & then add as much flour as needed to make dough soft enough to roll ¼ inch thick. Cut & bake in hot oven 15 min.

~ Comfort. May 1920

CHOCOLATE COOKIES

Fannie Merritt Farmer published the first chocolate Brownie recipe in her 1906 edition of the *Boston Cooking-School Cook Book*. Some say the recipe was a product of a failed cake, which is possible, though unlikely. However, some yummy results have come from baking chocolate pound cakes and other rich chocolate cakes so that they're "sad," or underdone. I postulate that someone came up with the dense, rich, chocolate cake bar on purpose, and the recipe became immediately popular with women, especially, whose passion for chocolate is no secret.

BROWNIES
Boston Cooking-School Cook Book, 1906

Over the years, brownie recipes have become richer and richer, but Miss Farmer's 1906 recipe is still darn good.

> 1 cup sugar
> ¾ teaspoon vanilla
> ¼ cup melted butter
> ½ cup flour
> 1 egg, unbeaten
> ½ cup walnut meats, cut in pieces
> 2 squares unsweetened chocolate, melted

Mix ingredients in order given. Line a seven-inch square pan with paraffine paper. Spread mixture evenly in pan and bake in a slow oven. As soon as taken from oven turn from pan, remove paper, and cut cake in strips, using a sharp knife. If these directions are not followed, paper will cling to cake, and it will be impossible to cut it in shapely pieces.

Chocolate Grater, 1905

CHOCOLATE COOKIES

9. BROWNES

1 cup butter, ½ square chocolate, (grated & melted together) 2 eggs beaten, 1 cup sugar added then put with the butter, & chocolatc, ½ cup flour (strong) 1 cup chopped nuts, 1 teaspoon vanilla. Spread thin, bake to a delicate brown in hot oven. Be careful not to over do, as scorching spoils chocolate.

Something's not right with this recipe. I think Anna was distracted when she recorded it. I'd say she meant to write ½ cup butter and 1 square of chocolate. Or maybe ½ square chocolate was half of a 4 oz. bar, which would be about right.

Strong Flour
New Home Cook Book, 1925

"Flour from spring wheat contains more gluten than that of winter wheat and is known as "strong" flour. Bread (strong) flour absorbs more moisture than flour made from winter wheat. Flour from winter wheat is lower in gluten and called soft wheat or pastry flour."

16. COCOA COOKIES

Cream ½ cup butter, 1 scant cup sugar, add 1 egg, ¼ cup milk, 2 cups flour, 4 teaspoons cocoa (dry), 1 teaspoon cinnamon, & 1 of salt. Roll out, cut & bake in moderate oven.

Well-known cookbook author, Maria Parloa published this recipe in *Miss Parloa's New Cook Book* in 1882. The cookies have a nice crunchy texture, a welcome change from the usual puffy soft 19th century fare. Only the combination of chocolate and cinnamon in this particular cookie tastes an awful lot like dirt. Not that we eat much dirt around here, but it's what I'd imagine dirt would taste like. The no. 41 Boston Brownies recipe is much better.

CHOCOLATE COOKIES

41. BOSTON BROWNIES

1 cup sugar, ⅓ cup butter, 2 eggs well beaten, 2 squares of bitter chocolate, 1 teaspoon baking powder, 1 cup nutmeats (broken) ½ cup raisins, 1 scant cup flour. Mix well & drop by teaspoon on waxed paper 2 inches apart. You can bake them in tiny cup cake tins placing an English walnut on each before putting in oven. Bake in moderate oven.

64. CHOCOLATE COOKIES

2 cups sugar, 1½ cups flour, ⅔ cup chocolate, ⅔ cup butter, 2 teaspoon vanilla, ½ cup milk, 3 eggs. Beat all well & drop in pan & bake.

"Cookey Pan" 1906

113. CHOCOLATE COOKIES

1 cup brown sugar, 1 cup granulated sugar, 1 cup butter, 1 egg, 1 cup grated chocolate, 1 teaspoon extract vanilla, & about 1½ cups flour stiff enough to roll. Roll very thin. Cut shape desired & bake a very short time.

207. CHOCOLATE NUT COOKIES

1 cup sugar, 2 tablespoons butter, 1 egg, 1¾ cup flour, 1 teaspoon soda, 3 teaspoons of cocoa or chocolate, & 1 teaspoon of cinnamon, ½ cup milk, 1 teaspoon baking powder, ½ cup chopped nuts, ½ cup raisins, 1 teaspoon vanilla. Mix all well & drop & bake in moderate oven.

July 25, 1919 from Comfort

PINWHEEL COOKIES

W itness the birth of pinwheel cookies. Right here before your very eyes, you can see how they came to be. First there was the marble cookie, two different but complementary doughs combined; one dropped on top of the other before baking. Then there was the swirled marble cookie with the two different doughs stirred slightly together. AND THEN...there was the ribbon cookie, which was a real live pinwheel cookie with two separate doughs rolled out flat, one on top of the other, then both rolled up together jelly roll style and sliced. Pinwheel cookies are a blast. Try combinations of two different doughs like chocolate and coconut or peanut butter or creme de menthe. Put fillings in the pinwheel like dates or chopped fresh cranberry orange or figs or apricots or ... anything! I've included a couple of recipes in addition to Anna's as these are such fun cookies.

Photo by Leon Swell

7. RIBBON COOKIES

Make white cookies after any receipt — flavoring with lemon; and chocklet cookies flavor with vanilla. Roll the latter thin; then roll the other the same way. Place one on the top of the other and roll up same as you would a jelly roll. With a sharp knife cut off slices, the usual thickness of cookies; lay them flat on baking pan & bake. (They are delicious & a little more trouble to make than the ordinary cookies.)

215. MARBLE COOKIES

Cream ¼ cup butter, add 1 cup brown sugar, beat well & add ½ cup of sweet milk, 1 beaten egg, 1 teaspoon vanilla, add 1¾ cup flour with 1½ teaspoons baking powder, & beat well. Now divide into 2 equal parts. Leave one part white & to the other part add these spices. 1 teaspoon cinnamon, ½ teaspoon allspice, ½ teaspoon mace. Drop white portion by small spoonfuls on greased baking tins, then drop a spoonful of dark mixture on the top of the white one. Bake 15 minutes in a hot oven.

From *Modern Priscilla*

PINWHEEL COOKIES

CHOCOLATE ORANGE MARBLED COOKIES
The People's Home Journal, March 1907

Anna copied some of her recipes from the People's Home Journal magazine and I'm sure if she had seen this one 10 years before she started her cookie book, she would have included it. My, my, my! This cookie is incredible! The recipe will work as written, but I tweaked it just a tad and substituted Grand Marnier for the orange juice.

"For delicious marbled cookies, cream one cupful of butter and two cupfuls of sugar. Add four well beaten eggs, then three scant cupfuls of flour sifted with two heaping teaspoonfuls of baking powder. Divide the batter in half. To one half add either one-half cupful or a cupful of grated chocolate, according to the preference, some people liking more and others less of this flavoring. To this other half, add the juice and grated rind of an orange. After flavoring both parts, combine them in one streaked lump of dough, and roll it very thin. Cut the dough into fancy cookies with diamond, heart-shaped and triangular cutters. Bake them in a rather hot oven. If the butter is fresh, add a pinch of salt."

CHOCOLATE ORANGE PINWHEEL COOKIES

1 cup butter	2½ cups flour
1¾ cup sugar	½ tsp. salt
2 eggs	1 tsp. baking powder
Rind of an orange, grated	3 Tbs. Grand Marnier liqueur
¾ cup semi-sweet chocolate chips, melted	

Cream butter and sugar, add eggs. Sift dry ingredients and add to creamed mixture. Divide the dough in half. To one half add melted chocolate chips, and to the other half, add the grated orange rind and Grand Marnier orange liqueur or equal amounts of orange juice. Mix as a marbled cookie or a pinwheel. Form into rolls, wrap with waxed paper and chill until firm. Slice thin and bake 10 minutes in a 350° oven. If you prefer a sweeter cookie, add ¼ cup more sugar.

PINWHEEL COOKIES

MOCHA PINWHEELS

½ cup butter	1½ cup flour
¾ cup sugar	¼ tsp. salt
1 egg	1 tsp. baking powder
1 tsp. hot water	1 oz. square unsweetened chocolate
1 tsp. vanilla	¼ tsp. cardamom (optional)
1 level Tbs. instant coffee	

Cream butter and sugar, add egg and vanilla, blend well. Sift flour, salt, and baking powder and add to butter mixture. Blend, then divide the dough in half. To one half add melted and cooled chocolate. To the other half, stir in cardamom, then coffee dissolved in as little hot water as possible. Chill both doughs. When firm, roll each flavor out onto a piece of lightly floured waxed paper into a rectangle shape as thin as you can get it, making sure both flavors are the same size. Now, flip the coffee over the chocolate and roll up, jelly-roll fashion. Refrigerate or freeze until firm, then slice about ¼ inch thick and bake in a 375° oven about 10 minutes until light brown.

Courtesy of the Library of Congress

•*When the lid of the stove falls on the floor, you are going to receive undeserved scandal.*
•*If the steam of the teakettle issues from the spout in short spurts, you will hear good news.* ~*Home Secrets*, 1898

WHOLE WHEAT COOKIES

The granola generation of the 1960's didn't invent "health cookies," though we can thank the hippies for re-popularizing earthy desserts. Baked goods made from graham (whole wheat flour) and wheat bran have graced the tables of the fiber-conscious for centuries, both in America and abroad. Known as "digestives" or wheatmeal biscuits in England, and graham cookies in the States, they can be a delicious as well as a healthy snack.

Peanut butter appears in recipe no. 167 Graham Cookies (page 94), and was a brand new "health food" at the time that Anna wrote her cookie book. It wouldn't be until the 1920's when the homogenization process introduced a palatable product that peanut butter would become a staple of American diets for young and old alike.

18. BRAN COOKIES

Cream together ½ cup butter, ⅔ cup brown sugar, 2 eggs, 2 tablespoons milk, ½ teaspoon salt, 1 cup white flour, & 2½ cups bran, 2 teaspoons baking-powder, all measures are level. An addition of ½ cup chopped raisins or dates is an improvement. Roll ¼ inch thick, or less, cut & bake in quick oven until delicately brown.

Whole Wheat Cookies

19. Graham Cookies

2 cups sugar, 2 heaping tablespoons butter, 2 eggs, (1 will do) 2 teaspoon cinnamon, pinch of salt, 2 cups sour milk, in which dissolve 2 teaspoons soda, 1 cup currants, & 3 cups graham flour, or enough to make a batter that will drop from a spoon. Drop on greased tins a little distance apart. These are extra good if a cup of chopped nut-meats is added, and very nutritious.

128. Graham Cookies

Mix 2 cups sugar, ½ cup lard (melted), 2 eggs. Add 2 cups sour milk, 2 level teaspoons soda, 2 cups graham flour, 1 cup white flour, & mix as for cookies. Roll out thin. Cut & bake in moderate oven.

"Edgar Kitchen, 13 yrs. old gets $3.25 a week driving the dairy wagon."

Photo by Lewis W. Hine, 1916   *Courtesy of the Library of Congress*

WHOLE WHEAT COOKIES

167. GRAHAM COOKIES

½ cup butter, or peanut butter, 1 cup sugar, 1 egg, & beat until light with 1 cup sugar added. Add 1 teaspoon soda dissolved in 2 tablespoons water, 2 tablespoons milk, about 3 cups of graham flour or enough to roll well. Roll out very thin, cut any shape desired. Bake in a moderate oven until thoroughly crisp & lightly brown, about 8 minutes.

I was totally ready to make fun of these cookies all over the place. Sure, they look funny and they're dry, and OK, they're downright mealy. But I can't stop eating them. What was healthy a hundred years ago is still healthy now, and these rustic, crunchy little whole wheat peanut butter cookies go great with my afternoon tea. So I think you should try them too. Share them with your special, adventurous friends. You know, the earthy ones who get a kick out of weeding their vegetable gardens and think getting dressed up means knocking the mud off of their boots and putting on a clean pair of overalls.

PEANUT BUTTER GRAHAMS

½ cup peanut butter
¾ to 1 cup brown sugar (depending on your sweet tooth)
1 egg
1 tsp. vanilla
1 tsp. soda dissolved in 1 Tbs. milk and 1 Tbs. water
2 cups whole wheat flour

Cream peanut butter and sugar, then beat in egg. Blend in vanilla and water/milk mixture. Stir in the flour and refrigerate at least an hour. When chilled, knead a minute, adding more flour if needed, roll out onto floured waxed paper ¼ inch thick into a triangle. Cut with a ridged pastry roller or knife into rectangles about 1½ inches by 2½ inches. Poke a couple sets of holes in each cookie with a fork. Bake at 350° for around 10 minutes until nicely browned.

Currant Grahams: These are really good, too. Substitute an equal amount of butter for the peanut butter and add about ½ cup currants. Sprinkle tops with a little coarse sugar and roll once with a rolling pin so it sinks in a bit. Mix and bake as above.

CORNMEAL COOKIES

42. CORN MEAL COOKIES

Put into a sifter 1½ cups of each of fine cornmeal & white flour, 2 teaspoons baking powder, 1 teaspoon salt, & sift twice. Cream together 1 cup sugar, 3 tablespoons of butter, 1 egg, 1 teaspoon vanilla, (or any spice liked) & ½ cup milk. Mix in dry ingredients & mix well adding more milk if necessary to make a dough of consistency to roll out well. Roll thin, cut with cookie cutter & bake in fairly hot oven to a delicate brown – about 10 minutes.

These cookies were a big hit this winter with a classroom of 4th graders at an Asheville, NC elementary school. I brought them in for some expert tasting advice as part of a presentation on Appalachian pioneers, and the kids gave them the ultimate rave review..."More!"

Because corn could be grown easily in the southern mountains around stumps and up the sides of steep land, corn products have been a staple of the mountaineer diet for the last 200 years. With wheat being a less popular crop, creative mountain cooks were able to make pie crusts, cookies, and cakes using cornmeal in place of white flour with great results. In addition, cornmeal would have been a good wheat substitute during World War I when Americans were asked to conserve white flour.

For Anna's cookies, buy finely ground cornmeal, but be sure you purchase plain meal and not self-rising. I get my cornmeal locally grown and stone-milled, and using half of this type of cornmeal in the recipe makes for too gritty a cookie, so I've altered the recipe a bit. (See pg. 96.)

Cornmeal Cookies

Barb's Cornmeal Cookies

Cornmeal crunchy and fragrant with lemon and butter, these just sweet enough cookies go great with a cup of afternoon tea.

¾ cup butter, softened
¾ cup white sugar
1 egg
1½ cups all-purpose flour
½ cup yellow cornmeal
½ tsp. baking powder
¼ tsp. salt
1 tsp. vanilla or ½ tsp. lemon extract
Grated zest of one lemon

Cream butter and sugar; add egg, vanilla, lemon zest and continue beating until blended. Sift together flour, cornmeal, baking powder and salt, then add to wet ingredients. Stir or beat until well blended. Form into a log and wrap tightly in plastic wrap. Refrigerate a couple of hours until firm. To bake, preheat oven to 375°. Slice cookies about ¼-inch thick and place on a greased cookie sheet, or on parchment paper. Bake about 10 minutes, just until edges are a light brown.

206. Corn Meal Hermits

Cream ¼ cup butter, add ⅓ cup light brown sugar & ⅓ cup corn syrup & mix well. Add ½ cup chopped raisins, 1 egg (well beaten), & 2 tablespoons of milk. Mix & sift 1¼ cups flour, ¾ cup fine corn meal, 2 teaspoons baking powder, ½ teaspoon cinnamon, ¼ teaspoon cloves, & ¼ teaspoon nutmeg. Mix all well & drop with spoon on greased baking sheet & bake in rather a quick oven.

OATMEAL COOKIES

King Ferdinand was an honest, hard-working, stubborn man. He believed that his somewhat puny people needed to refrain from using alcohol and tobacco products and eat more oats. During his reign as "Cereal King" from the 1870's to 1899, Ferdinand Schumacher of Ohio transformed oats from horse food to America's favorite breakfast cereal.

In 1851, Schumacher immigrated from Germany to Akron, where he opened up a small grocery. Oats had long been recognized as a healthy food in Europe and he thought they'd make Americans stronger, too. So he chopped them up and sold the oats in little jars which, surprisingly, folks took to like crazy. In 1876 Schumacher invented a method of heating the oats and flattening them by feeding them through rollers, and that's when the cereal really took off. When his mill tragically burned in 1886, Schumacher's neighboring oat miller convinced him to form a partnership which would eventually become the American Cereal Company as other millers joined forces.

The American Cereal Company's Quaker Oats were packaged in square boxes, advertised, and began appearing in breads and cookies by the time the Quaker Oats Company was formed in 1901. Quick cooking oats, made from chopping the oat groat into several pieces before flattening on rollers, wouldn't appear on the market until the 1920's, so the fine oats called for in Anna's recipes must be pin oats, or chopped steel cut oats, which are also known as Scottish Oats.

The Final Fruit
Of the Oat Field
Is the Well-Fed, Energetic Child

OATMEAL COOKIES

1. FILLED OATMEAL COOKIES

2 cups rolled oats, 3 cups flour, 1 teaspoon salt, 2 cups sugar, 1 cup shortning, 1 cup sour milk with 1 teaspoon soda dissolved in the milk. Cream the sugar & shortning, mix flour, oat meal, & salt & add milk. Mix stiff & roll very thin. Cut with cookie cutter & on each one put a teaspoon of prunes & raisins cooked together. Cover with another cookie & press edges together.

Being fresh out of prunes, I made the filling for this cookie out of dried sour cherries and all I can say is wowee! This is THE BEST cookie I have ever eaten. I thought Anna had accidently left the egg out of the recipe, but I think this is supposed to be an eggless cookie. They have it all ... crunchy, chewy, tart, nutty, buttery, earthy, wholesome, rustic, big, and they are lookers. I'm entering them in the fair this year, and I plan to win. That's how good they are. (See recipe, right.)

This is not a beginner cookie, but don't be afraid to try them if you are. They're just difficult to roll and cut. My last cookbook was on pie baking, and though I've become somewhat of a dough rolling queen, I had a bit of a challenge cutting out these cookies. You'll just need to practice if it doesn't work the first time. They're worth the suffering! Here's half a recipe that makes 13 giant cookies. They will spread quite a bit as they bake.

A young girl feeds a horse oats from her apron, 1906

Courtesy of the Library of Congress

OATMEAL COOKIES

SOUR CHERRY AMARETTO WALNUT FILLED OATMEAL COOKIES

½ cup brown sugar
½ cup white sugar
½ cup butter
¼ cup buttermilk

½ tsp. soda
½ tsp. salt (scant)
1 cup flour
1¼ cups rolled oats

Photo by Wes Erbsen

Cream sugars and butter. Mix soda and buttermilk and blend with sugar mixture. Sift flour and salt and add to creamed mixture. Stir in oats. Refrigerate at least 2 hours. Take out half the dough and return rest to refrigerator. Flour your board, as Anna says, and knead your dough just a bit until it holds together enough to roll, adding a bit more flour if needed. Roll the dough out as thin as you can get it between two layers of floured waxed paper. If the paper won't peel off, freeze dough for a few minutes. The key to success is in keeping your dough chilled. You should be able to cut out about 12 or 13 two-inch circles. Place the circles on parchment paper, or buttered tin, and put a teaspoon of filling on each round. Now, cut out the remaining dough circles. Cover each circle, press edges together lightly, and punch a hole in the top (with a chopstick or your finger) so you can see how pretty the filling is through the cookie. Bake at 375° about 12 minutes until they're a nice brown.

Filling:

¾ cup dried sour cherries
⅓ cup water
¼ cup sugar
⅓ cup walnuts coarsely cut
⅓ lemon, juice and yellow rind
3 Tbs. Amaretto (almond) liqueur

Slice the yellow rind (no white) from the lemon and chop up. Simmer cherries, sugar, lemon rind, and water together on low about 5 minutes until soft. Whirl in blender a few seconds. Add walnuts, lemon juice and Amaretto. Let filling cool to room temperature before using.

OATMEAL COOKIES

2. OATMEAL COOKIES

Cream 1 cup butter; 1 cup sugar; dissolve 1 teaspoon soda & 1 teaspoon salt in 3 tablespoons of boiling water; & add cold water enough to make ½ cup; & then mix with the above sugar & etc. Have ready 3 cups rolled oats; mixed with 3 cups of flour. Add part to the mixture & when smooth add remainder. This makes a dry dough but do not add any moisture. Press raisins in cookies this way. Picture in Comfort.

Many of Anna's recipes came from "*Comfort.*" After searching for towns by that name, I realized she was referring to a women's magazine claiming to be "*The Key to Happiness and Success in Over a Million and a Quarter Homes.*"

13. OATMEAL COOKIES

½ lb. flour, 6 oz. sugar, 1 egg, ½ teaspoon cinnamon, ½ lb. chopped raisins, ½ lb. rolled oats, 6 oz. butter, ½ gill of milk, 1 teaspoon soda, 1 of salt. Mix well all dry ingredients, then add the eggs well beatten & the milk. Drop small teaspoons of the mixture on a baking tin, taking care they are not very close together; & bake till done in moderately hot oven.

17. GRIDLY OATMEAL COOKIES

1¼ cup sugar, 1 cup butter, 1 egg, 1 cup chopped raisins, 1 teaspoon cinnamon, 1 level teaspoon soda dissolved in a little vinegar, 2 cups oat meal (not rolled oats), 1½ cups flour, 1 cup sour cream or buttermilk. Drop by small spoonfuls into tins & bake.

Oatmeal Cookies

15. Rolled Oat Cookies

¾ cup butter, 1 cup sugar, 2 eggs, ½ cup chopped nuts, ¾ teaspoon soda, 2 teacups rolled oats, 1 cup chopped raisins, 1 teaspoon cinnamon, 2 cups flour, pinch of salt. Cream butter, sugar, add eggs, cinnamon, salt & soda. Mix well & add raisins & nuts. Mix well again, then add the flour, & lastly rolled oats. When all is well mixed, drop by teaspoon on well greased pan, 3 inches apart. Bake in a moderate oven. Will remain fresh for weeks.

Also referred to as "Boston Cookies" in the 1911 *Inglenook Cook Book*, recipe contributor Sister Brubaker was not thrilled with the looks of these cookies. She said: "This does not make very pretty cakes, but they are very palatable if let set a couple of days before using."

24. Oat Meal Fancies

2 cups rolled oats, 2 cups pastry flour, 1 teaspoon salt, 1 teaspoon soda, 1 cup raisins, cut, ⅔ cup lard, 1 cup brown sugar, 2 eggs, 1 cup warm water, & 1 teaspoon vanilla. Mix well together, & drop by spoon on greased tin. Bake in rather quick oven.

Courtesy of the Library of Congress

OATMEAL COOKIES

HOOSIER

31. OAT MEAL DROPS

1 cup each of sugar, butter, oatmeal (not rolled oats) & 1 cup raisins or nuts, 2 eggs, 1 teaspoon cinnamon, 1 teaspoon soda, 3 tablespoons sour milk, 2 cups flour and flavoring.

Toddlers will enjoy this easygoing cookie (minus the raisins and nuts). Here's a jazzed-up version you adults will love. Quick cooking oats lend a light texture to these wonderfully crisp, rustic cookies.

BRANDIED RAISIN OATMEAL DROPS

½ cup white sugar	2 Tbs. sour milk or yogurt
1 cup brown sugar	2 cups quick cooking oats
1 cup butter	2 cups flour
2 eggs	½ tsp. salt
1 tsp. vanilla	1 tsp. baking soda
¾ cup raisins	¾ cup chopped walnuts
¼ cup brandy or rum	

Soak raisins in warm brandy until plump. Cream sugar and butter, add eggs, vanilla, and sour milk. Sift together flour, salt, and soda and add to creamed mixture. Stir in oats, raisins and any remaining brandy, and walnuts. Drop by spoonful onto paper or greased cookie sheet. Sprinkle quick oats over tops and bake in a 350° oven about 10 minutes until medium brown.

Note: If you don't have sour milk, cream, or yogurt, substitute a teaspoon of baking powder for the soda and add an equal amount of milk, though your end product will be a bit different.

OATMEAL COOKIES

53. OAT MEAL COOKIES

1 cup shortning, 2 cups sugar, 2 eggs, 1 teaspoon soda dissolved in 1 tablespoon of hot water, 2 cups oat meal, 2 cups flour, 1 teaspoon baking powder, 2 cups chopped raisins, 1 teaspoon cinnamon. Mix all well and bake. (leave out baking powder and use 1 cup brown sugar and 1 cup white sugar)

175. ROLLED OAT FRUIT DROPS

Two fourths cup shortning, 1 cup sugar, 2 eggs, 1½ cups flour, ½ teaspoon salt, 1⅛ teaspoon cinnamon. Add 2 cups rolled oats, ¾ cup seeded raisins, ⅔ cup English walnuts broken in pieces. Mix well & dissolve ¾ teaspoon soda in 2 tablespoons hot water. Mix all well & drop from teaspoon. Bake in hot oven 5 minutes. **Note:** How 'bout the two fourths!!!

189. OATMEAL DROP COOKIES

Cream ¾ cup butter with 1 cup light brown sugar, add 2 eggs, & 4 tablespoons sweet milk. Stir in 2 cups rolled oats & when these are well moistened, add 1 cup flour, sifted with 1 level teaspoon soda & salt, cinnamon, cloves, & nutmeg to taste. Best add 1 teaspoon cinnamon & ½ teaspoon of other spices each. Drop from spoon on buttered pan allowing room to spread. If cookies spread too much in baking, add more flour.

192. ROLLED OAT ROCKS COOKIES

Cream ½ cup butter with 1 cup sugar. Add 2 eggs, ⅔ cup sour milk, pinch salt, 2 cups rolled oats, 2 cups flour, ½ cup cleaned currants, 1 cup raisins, spices to taste, & 1 teaspoon soda. Mix & drop by teaspoon on greased tins & bake in hot oven 10 minutes.

OATMEAL COOKIES

198. OAT MEAL COOKIES

1 egg, ¼ cup sugar, ¼ cup sweet cream, ¼ cup milk, ½ cup fine oatmeal, 2 cups flour, 2 teaspoons baking powder, 1 teaspoon salt. Beat egg till light, add sugar, cream, milk, then these to oat meal, flour, powder & salt mixed & sifted. Toss on floured board, roll thin, cut, and bake in moderate oven.

Blegg! Not good. Closer scrutiny tells me these are really an Americanized version of Scottish oatcakes, which are really quite good with a slab of your favorite cheese. So here's a recipe I recently picked up in England for a British version of Scottish oatcakes that resembles Anna's Cookie. Like the recipe above, they're more of a cracker, not a cookie. Don't tell anybody, but I'd rather eat one of these oatcakes than a cookie.

OATCAKES

1½ cup fine oatmeal (pinhead or quick)
⅓ cup flour
½ tsp. soda
½ tsp. salt
1 Tbs. brown sugar (optional)
1½ Tbs. melted butter
Hot Water (about ½ cup)
Extra oatmeal for rolling

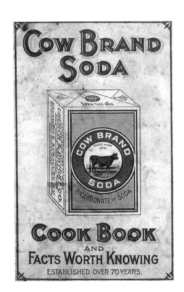

Mix dry ingredients together in a bowl, then add melted butter and enough hot water to form a stiff dough. Knead lightly and roll out as thin as you can onto a board sprinkled with oatmeal. Cut with a round cutter and bake at 350° for about 15-20 minutes. They should only be a pale color, not brown. Oatcakes are traditionally baked on a girdle (iron griddle), and that makes me wonder if these should have been called "gridly oatmeal cookies" instead of Anna's no. 17 recipe on page 100.

OATMEAL COOKIES

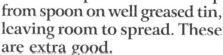

170. ROLLED OAT COOKIES

Mix ¾ cup butter, 1 cup sugar, 2 eggs, 1 teaspoon cinnamon, pinch salt, ¾ teaspoon soda. Mix well & add 1 cup chopped raisins, ½ cup chopped nuts, mix well again, then add 2 cups flour, 2 cups rolled oats (scant). Mix well again & drop from teaspoon on well buttered pans about 3 inches apart. Bake in moderate oven. Will remain fresh for weeks.

210. OAT MEAL COOKIES

Cream ⅔ cup shortning with 1 heaping cup sugar, add 1 egg, ⅓ cup milk, 1 teaspoon each of soda & vanilla, a little nutmeg & pinch of salt, 2 cups rolled oats that have been run through a food chopper, & 2½ cups flour. A cup each of raisins & nutmeats improves them. Drop from spoon on well greased tin, leaving room to spread. These are extra good.

220. COLONIAL COOKIES

½ cup granulated sugar, ½ cup brown sugar, ¾ cup shortning, ½ cup sour cream, ½ cup boiling water, ¾ cup rolled oats, 4 cups flour, 1 egg yolk, 1 teaspoon baking soda, 1 teaspoon salt, ½ cup each of raisins & walnuts, 1 teaspoon vanilla. Cream shortning & sugar, add egg yolk & cream. Scald rolled oats with boiling water & add with flour & fruit. Chill (put in ice chest), roll on board. Less flour may be used, have dough as soft as can be handled. Bake in a moderate oven. Keep in Crock. Improves with age. *Modern Priscilla*

COCONUT COOKIES

Sometime in the 1940's, Americans changed the spelling of co-coanut to coconut. If you enjoy re-creating vintage recipes, the older spelling not only gives you an idea of the recipe's age, but you will also have some indication of what kind of coconut to use. Anna had a choice of either fresh coconut or dried (which would have been reconstituted by soaking in milk about 30 minutes). Coconut season is October to December, but they keep for at least a few months at room temperature. I'm guessing Anna would have made her cookies with fresh coconut from October to April and dried coconut the rest of the year.

After you grate up your knuckles working on a fresh coconut, the frozen product will start to look pretty good. But, scraped knuckles aside, there's nothing as good as a fresh coconut cookie. Here's how you prepare a fresh coconut. First, choose one with plenty of liquid inside. Then poke a hole in a couple of the eyes and drain out the milk. Bake it in a 350° oven for about 20 minutes. Wrap the coconut in a dish towel and crack it lightly with a hammer in several places. Remove the shell and use a potato peeler or a paring knife to remove the skin. Skin removal is the hardest part.

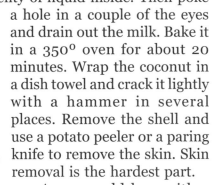

Anna would have either used a hand grater, or she would have just chopped up the coconut real fine. I say stick it in a food processor and use your shredding attachment. A fresh coconut will yield about 4 cups unpacked grated coconut. The high fat meat goes rancid quickly, so you can freeze whatever you don't need for a recipe in one-cup packages. To toast, spread on a cookie sheet and bake in a 325° oven until lightly browned. Stir coconut occasionally and whatever you do, don't let it scorch!

Coconut Cookies

Quick Way to Prepare Cocoanut

To prepare fresh cocoanut for any use, in place of using the grater in the old way, just put the cocoanut through the meat chopper. It comes out light and fluffy, and can be done in a few seconds; and best of all, you have no bruised and bleeding fingers from using the grater.
~The Modern Priscilla, Oct. 1915

Enterprise Meat Grinder

23. Cocoanut and Oat Meal Cookies

1 cup butter, 3 eggs, 1 large cup milk, 1 cup each of cocoanut & oatmeal, 3 teaspoons baking powder, 1 teaspoon each of salt & lemon extract, & flour to roll. Addition of a cup of raisins is very good.

46. Cocoanut Balls or Cookies

If fresh cocoanut is not available, use dried first soaking in all the fresh milk it will absorb. To each 2 cups of cocoa-nut add 1 cup sugar, powdered preferable. Add 2 tablespoons flour, & white of an egg well beaten stiff. Mix well, shape into balls, roll in powdered sugar & bake in slow oven 20 minutes. To make cookies, just flatten the balls.

61. Cocoanut Cream Cookies

1 cup sugar, 2 eggs, ½ cup shredded cocoanut, 1 cup thick cream, & 3 cups flour, 3 teaspoons baking powder & 1 teaspoon salt. Roll out ½ inch thick, sprinkle with cocoanut, roll thin, cut with cutter dipped in flour. Bake in moderate oven.

COCONUT COOKIES

158. COCOANUT COOKIES

1 cup butter, 2 cups sugar, 2 eggs, 1 cup grated cocoanut, 2 teaspoons baking powder, flour enough to roll. Roll very thin, bake quickly, but do not brown.

216. COCOANUT PASTRY COOKIES

Delicious cookies can be made by utilizing the trimmings left over when making pie crust. Knead the scraps together, roll out again, sprinkle with sugar & cocoanut, fold up & roll out once more. Cut in squares or rounds with cookie cutter. Lay on well greased tin & bake until light brown. These little cookies will keep a long time if placed in an air tight tin box.

Paste Jagger

217. COCOANUT COOKIE JUMBLES

Mix together 2 cups sugar, 1 cup butter, 2 cups flour, 1 teaspoon baking powder, pinch salt, & 1 small cup of shredded cocoanut. Beat 2 eggs & mix all together. Drop in well buttered pans & bake a light brown.

Tasty, buttery, crunchy cookies. Do make them! An almost identical recipe can be found in the 1915 *Larkin Housewives Cook Book*. This recipe assumes you will be using fresh grated coconut. If you substitute packaged sweetened cocoanut, decrease sugar by at least ¼ cup, and pack a regular cup measure with the cocoanut. Designed to be dropped, they're especially good as icebox cookies. Just add ½ cup more flour and form into logs. Wrap in waxed paper, freeze, and slice thinly to bake. Bake in a 375° oven about 8-10 minutes until lightly browned. As Anna would say, "a teaspoon of vanilla improves them."

Macaroons & Kisses

C ookies made with beaten egg whites, sugar, flavorings, and nuts have been enjoyed in Europe and elsewhere for centuries. Anna's selection of macaroons (with ground nuts and coconut) and kisses (meringues) hadn't changed much in the 70-plus years before she recorded them. In an era before electric kitchen appliances, we're left to ponder, how did Anna whip the air into her egg whites, and what about her mother, grandmother, great-grandmother?

The cast iron "New and Improved Egg Beater" was patented by the Monroe brothers in 1859. In the decades that followed, inventors produced a slew of creative hand-held gadgets that quickly whipped air into egg whites, and cream as well. Rufus Eastman would patent a powered mixer in 1885 that could be run by mechanical, water, or electric power, but electric mixers weren't commonplace in American homes until the 1930's. Although Anna would have had lots of choices of egg beating gadgets to choose from in the 1910's, she likely did her whipping with something similar to this Dover rotary beater.

48. Kisses

Beat whites of 6 eggs, 6 tablespoons powdered sugar on warm stove till it will draw like a rope string from spoon. Flavor with vanilla & add 1 cup of course chopped almonds or other nuts. Mix all well & drop with teaspoon on well buttered baking sheet a little apart. Bake in slow oven as they should dry rather than bake. Leave them in oven 1 hour or longer. Bake light brown.

55. Cocoanut Drops or Kisses

Grate small cocoanut or ½ of one, according to the amount you want to make. Add to it half its weight in sugar (use less if less sweet desired). Add white of 1 egg, beaten stiff. Mix well & drop by teaspoon well apart. Bake in hot oven 15 minutes being careful not to scorch. If liked, flavor with any good flavoring.

MACAROONS & KISSES

Kisses, 1906

MACAROONS & KISSES

91. MACAROONS COOKIES

1 lb. sweet almonds, (blanched & beaten to a paste), mix with them 1¼ lbs. powdered sugar, the grated rind of 2 lemons, & the whites of 6 eggs. Drop on buttered paper & bake a light brown in a moderate oven.

QUICK AND TASTY ALMOND MACAROONS

It's easy enough to buy a can of almond paste and make some delicious almond macaroons, but the old-fashioned way is even better. If you like almonds, a cookie doesn't get any better than this light, sweet morsel with a chewy inside.

½ lb. blanched almonds	3 egg whites
1 cup sugar	½ tsp. almond extract

Process almonds in food processor fitted with steel blade until almost a paste. Add sugar and blend well. Beat egg whites in a separate bowl until stiff peaks are formed. Fold egg whites and extract into almond mixture. Drop onto parchment paper and bake at 375° for 8-10 minutes until tops are lightly browned.

132. MACAROONS COOKIES

2 cups hickory nut meats, beat fine in mortar. Add 2 cups sugar, 4 tablespoons flour, & 3 well beaten egg whites. Mix all well together & bake on greased paper. Put only little bit of this mixture in each place well apart. Bake very very slowly. These are also called kisses.

DR. CHAUNCEY'S PATENT
AIR TIGHT

COOKING STOVES

159. HICKORY NUT KISSES

Whites of 6 eggs beaten stiff, 1 lb. powdered sugar, 2 tablespoons flour & 1 lb. hickory-nut kernels. Drop on well buttered tins & bake in slow oven.

MACAROONS & KISSES

Cookies for Mr. Fetch

"Go entertain your company," Maw told Lis. "Fix your hair up a little."

218. COCOANUT MACAROONS

Beat the whites of 2 eggs stiff. Add slowly 1 cup powdered sugar, & 1 cup of grated cocoanut. Mix thoroughly & drop on buttered tins & bake slowly.

219. COCOANUT KISSES

Beat the whites of 4 eggs stiff. Add ⅔ cup of sugar, gradually while beating constantly, until mixture will hold its shape. Then cut & fold in ⅓ cup of fine gra. sugar, ⅓ cup of shredded cocoanut & ½ teaspoon vanilla. Drop by teaspoon and shape into rounds on a wet board covered with letter paper. Sprinkle with cocoanut & bake in a slow oven 30 minutes. Nut meats may be substituted for cocoanut, but meringues are satisfactory if neither is used.

Recipes 218 and 219 are close to how we make Kisses today. Beat egg whites until frothy, then add ¼ tsp. cream of tartar (to stabilize the whites). Gradually add 1 cup of sugar, beating until stiff peaks are formed and the sugar is dissolved. Stir in coconut and vanilla and bake on parchment paper in 250° oven about an hour until lightly browned.

PEANUT COOKIES

"How far you go in life depends on your being tender with the young, compassionate with the aged, sympathetic with the striving, and tolerant of the weak and the strong. Because someday in life you will have been all of these."

So says my all-time favorite hero, George Washington Carver. His most well-known contributions came during his years spent as the Director of Agriculture at Tuskegee Institute from 1897 until his death in 1943. There he developed a crop rotation method that would forever change southern farming. Dr. Carver didn't stop there, he invented hundreds of uses for the very crops that would enrich the soils so depleted from cotton farming over the years. And then he educated the public, for the benefit of all, as to why they needed to make use of these crops, such as soybeans, peanuts, pecans and sweet potatoes.

His accomplishments were seemingly endless, but we're here to talk about peanuts, and Dr. Carver was no slouch where peanut research was concerned. In his 1916 agricultural research bulletin *How to Grow the Peanut and 105 Ways of Preparing it for Human Consumption,* he encouraged Americans to eat this healthy, soil-enriching legume in every way you could possibly imagine. Not the least of which was in peanut cookies. Anna's Peanut Cookie Drops recipe is the same as that of Dr. Carver's Peanut Cookies #2.

37. PEANUT COOKIE DROPS
4 tablespoonfuls butter, 1 cup sugar, 2 eggs, 4 tablespoonfuls of milk, 2 teaspoons baking powder, 2 cups flour & 1 cup ground peanuts.

Here's a crunchier version with a more intense peanut flavor if that's your fancy.

> **4 tablespoons butter, softened**
> **¾ cup sugar (half of it brown sugar)**
> **1 egg**
> **1 tsp. vanilla**
> **1 tsp. baking powder**
> **1 cup flour**
> **1 cup ground lightly salted peanuts**

Note: To grind nuts, use an old timey nut grinder or whirl in food processor until pieces are small but not mealy.

Peanut Cookies

40. One Egg Peanut Cookies
Cream 2 tablespoons butter, ½ cup sugar, & 1 egg. To 1 cup flour, add ½ teaspoon soda, 1 teaspoon cream of tartar, mix & add 2 tablespoon of milk, & 1 cup chopped peanuts. Drop from teaspoon on buttered pans & bake.

59. Bermuda Peanut Wafer Cookies
Cream 2 tablespoons butter, ¼ cup sugar, 1 egg. Mix & sift ½ cup flour, 1 teaspoon baking powder, & ¼ teaspoon salt. Add to the first mixture, then add 2 tablespoons of milk & ½ cup chopped peanuts. Drop from teaspoon on baking sheet ½ inch apart & place ½ peanut on top of each. Bake in moderate oven from 12 to 15 minutes. This recipe will make 24 cookies.

81. Peanut Cookies
¼ cup butter, ½ cup sugar, 1 egg, 2 tablespoons milk, 1 cup flour, ¼ teaspoon salt, 2 teaspoons baking powder, ¾ cup shelled peanuts. Drop by teaspoon on greased pans & bake.

PEANUT COOKIES

169. PEANUT SNAPS

Mix 1½ cups butter & 2 cups sugar smooth. Add 6 eggs (beaten), 1½ pints flour, ½ cup corn starch, 1 teaspoon baking powder, 1 teaspoon extract of lemon. Flour the board, roll out the dough rather thin, cut cookies out, roll in chopped peanuts and sugar (about 1½ cups chopped peanuts with ½ cup sugar), lay on greased baking tin & bake in quick oven 8 or ten minutes.

Same cookie, a bit easier to make:

1½ sticks butter	1½ cup flour
1 cup sugar	¼ cup corn starch
1 egg	½ tsp. baking powder
½ cup chopped peanuts mixed with ¼ cup sugar	
½ tsp. lemon extract and/or grated rind of half a lemon	

Chill dough until firm, then roll out about ¼ inch thick onto waxed paper lightly sprinkled with flour. Cut with a biscuit cutter. Take away excess dough leaving only the cut circles. Sprinkle with some of the peanut/sugar mixture and lightly roll in with a rolling pin. Place cookies on parchment paper, peanut side down, then sprinkle the insides of each cookie with a little more of the mixture. Fold cookies over and bake at 375° for about 10 minutes until lightly browned, or you can leave them flat and bake.

187. PEANUT BUTTER COOKIES

1 cup sugar, ¾ cup peanut butter, ¼ cup sweet milk, 2 eggs, 1 ½ teaspoons baking powder & flour enough to roll. Do not use salt, flavoring or spice. Children are very fond of these cookies for school lunches, & they are very wholesome.

George Washington Carver

"He could have added fortune to fame but caring for neither, he found happiness and honor in being helpful to the world."

~Epitaph on George Washington Carver's grave

OTHER NUTS COOKIES

54. NUT COOKIES

½ cup almonds, ½ cup English walnuts, 1 cup dates, all chopped. 1 cup sugar, 6 tablespoons milk, 1 teaspoon vanilla, 2 eggs, 1 cup flour, 1 teaspoon baking powder. Roll out, cut & bake 20 minutes in a moderate oven.

56. NUT BARS

½ cup nuts, 1 cup dates chopped fine, 1 cup sugar, 1 cup flour, 1 teaspoon baking powder, 6 tablespoons milk, 1 teaspoon vanilla, 2 beaten eggs. Cut in bars, roll in sugar, & bake 20 minutes.

82. PAPA'S COOKIES

½ cup butter, 1½ cups sugar, 2 eggs, pinch salt, 2 cups flour, 2 cups chopped walnuts. Mix as usual, adding nuts last & a little milk to thin the batter. Drop from spoon well apart on greased tins or waxed paper & bake in rather quick oven. They should be crisp.

OTHER NUTS COOKIES

63. SPOONIE COOKIES (ALMOND)

1 ½ cups butter, 1 ½ cups sugar, 2 eggs, 4 cups flour, 2 teaspoons baking powder, ¼ lb. almonds. Roll thin & make small cookies. Rub white of an egg over the top and sprinkle chopped almonds on.

90. NUT JUMBLES COOKIES

½ cup butter, 1 cup sugar, 1 egg, 2 cups flour, pinch salt, 1 teaspoon baking powder, ⅓ cup milk, ¾ cup nut meats, (chopped course). Mix in the nuts well & drop in spoonfuls on greased pans, some distance apart. Bake in quick oven about 10 minutes.

102. ALMOND DROPS

6 eggs, 1 lb. sugar, ½ lb. butter, 1 quart flour, 2 teaspoon baking powder, 1 cup cream, 1 teaspoon extract almond. Drop from spoon on buttered paper.

107. ALMOND COOKIES

1 cup butter, 1 ½ cups sugar, 2 eggs, 1 cup sour cream, 1 teaspoon soda, 1 teaspoon extract of almond; flour enough to roll. Do not roll too thin.

165. ALMOND COOKIES

Mix 1 tablespoon butter, ½ cup gra. sugar, yolks of 2 eggs, add flour with baking powder enough to roll out. Cut cookies out, put in pan & glaze cookies with white of an egg & sprinkle with chopped almonds & granulated sugar. Bake in moderate oven.

172. WALNUT DROP COOKIES

½ lb. brown sugar, ½ lb broken walnut meats, 2 level tablespoons flour, ¼ teaspoon baking powder, ⅓ teaspoon salt, & 2 eggs. Mix all well & drop small spoonfuls on buttered pans, bake in quick oven.

174. ALMOND COOKIES

½ cup butter, 1 cup sugar, 1 egg, ⅓ cup almonds (blanched & finely chopped), 1 cup flour, 1 cup rolled oats, ¼ teaspoon cloves, ⅛ teaspoon salt, ½ teaspoon cinnamon, ½ teaspoon nutmeg & grated rind of a lemon, 2 teaspoons baking powder (mixed with flour). Add 2 tablespoons sherry wine. Drop from teaspoon well apart. Press ½ almond in center of each & bake in a moderate oven 12-15 minutes.

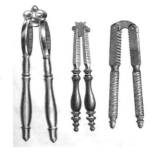

Oh, my! What an unexpected treat. Exotic and simple all at the same time, the heavenly scent of these snappy cookies will knock you sideways. I made a couple of adjustments below. Follow directions above, but lightly toast almonds before chopping.

½ cup butter	¾ cup flour
1 egg	⅛ tsp. salt
⅓ cup almonds	½ tsp. cinnamon
½ cup white sugar	½ tsp. nutmeg
½ cup brown sugar	¼ tsp. cloves
2 Tbs. sherry	1 tsp. baking powder
Grated rind of a lemon	1 cup rolled oats

This is GOOD storage

WAFERS

Want people to think you're a great cookie baker? Whip up a batch of these delicate, lacy, buttery, crispy beauties and you will be everybody's new best friend. The perfect bake sale cookie, the recipes cost little to make and will produce dozens of cookies. Anna only included a few wafer-type cookie recipes in her book, but I'm sneaking in a couple more because once you start making these, your friends won't want you to stop. They take a little practice to get right. I always recommend that you try a test cookie when

Courtesy of the Library of Congress

trying out any new recipe, but with wafers you really need to because the moisture level of the dough is crucial to a successful outcome. Parchment paper is a must, as well as storing the cooled cookies in an airtight container to maintain their crunch. All varieties of wafers freeze great up to 6 months.

62. WAFERS — ENGLISH ROLLED COOKIES

Heat ½ cup molasses, to boiling point, add ½ cup butter, then add slowly stirring constantly 1 cup flour scant, mixed & sifted with 1 tablespoon ginger, ⅔ cup sugar. Drop small portions from tip of spoon on a greased pan 2 inches apart. Bake in a slow oven, cool slightly, remove from pan & roll over handle of a wooden spoon. They are nice with 1 ½ cups of rolled oats added.

A European brandy snap without the brandy and using molasses instead of golden syrup. If not adding oats, you may need to add an additional ¼ cup flour. Bake at 300° for about 12 minutes until flattened and brown. Follow directions for brandy snaps (next page) for rolling.

WAFERS

BRANDY SNAPS

½ cup butter
½ cup brown sugar
¼ cup white sugar

¼ cup honey
1 cup flour
2 Tbs. brandy

Cream butter and sugar. Add honey and brandy, blend. Stir in flour. You will need to bake a test cookie so you see how your dough will behave. Drop by teaspoonful well apart onto parchment paper. Bake at 350° for about 8-10 minutes. The cookies will become flat and medium brown with little lacy holes throughout. Let cool about 1 minute until you can handle, then quickly wrap each cookie loosely around the handle of a wooden spoon. If the cookies cool so that you can't mold them, just return to oven until softened. Each flour absorbs moisture a little differently, so you may have to add more brandy if the snaps crack when you try to roll them.

Maple Brandy Snaps: Substitute maple syrup for the honey.
Chocolate Brandy Snaps: Dip the end of the rolled cookies in melted semi-sweet chocolate chips.
Brandy Snap Ice Cream Bowls: Instead of rolling the snaps, make them larger when baking and form into little bowls by molding them over the bottom of a muffin pan while warm. Serve filled with your favorite ice cream.

From left to right:
Cherry Shortbreads, pg. 50
Brandy Snaps Wafers, above
Icebox Anise Cookies, pg. 123

WAFERS

AUNT ADA'S OATMEAL LACE COOKIES

My Great Aunt Ada of Clarksburg, West Virginia, wasn't really a sunny, child-loving, cookie-lady type of a woman. She was more of a garden-digging, fiesty, outdoorsy, beautiful, smart woman. As kids, my sisters and I never quite knew what to make of her, but whenever we visited, she always warmed our hearts as well as our bellies with a pretty plateful of her oatmeal cookies. This recipe makes a ton of cookies; you can easily halve it.

1 cup brown sugar	¾ cup flour
1 cup white sugar	1 tsp. soda
1 cup butter	1 scant tsp. salt
2 eggs	3 cups old-fashioned rolled oats
1 tsp. vanilla	½ cup chopped walnuts (optional)

Cream butter and sugar, add eggs and beat. Add vanilla. Sift flour, salt, and soda and blend with creamed mixture. Stir in oats and walnuts. Drop by spoonful far apart onto parchment paper and bake at 350° about 10-12 minutes until flattened and lightly browned. When cool, store in airtight container so they stay crisp

BENNE SEED WAFERS

Benne or sesame seed wafers are a southern classic. While traditional Benne Seed Wafers are small cookies, this recipe from a 1950's Pawley's Island (Charleston, S.C.) cookbook makes tons of big-spreading lacy wafers. Hulled sesame seeds are inexpensive when bought unpackaged at organic markets. To toast, toss seeds into a cast iron frying pan and shake frequently over medium heat until light brown and fragrant, about 3-5 minutes. Cool before adding to batter.

½ cup butter	¾ cup flour
1½ cups brown sugar	½ tsp. soda
1 egg	¼ tsp. salt
1 tsp. vanilla	¾ cup toasted sesame seeds

Cream butter and sugar, add egg and vanilla; blend well. Sift dry ingredients and add to creamed mixture. Stir in sesame seeds. Drop by teaspoonful onto parchment paper and bake at 350° for 5-7 minutes. They're done when flattened and medium brown. Keep an eye on them as they burn quickly. Store in airtight container when cooled.

Interesting Flavors

While 19th century urban pharmacists were busy mixing up herbal remedies for the sick, they concocted flavoring extracts that could be added to soda water to keep their waiting customers happy. That explains not only how flavoring extracts were invented but also how the drugstore soda fountain came to be. But what about country folks who didn't live near a pharmacy? Patent medicine manufacturers relied on traveling salesmen to peddle their tonics, liniments, spices and extracts to rural America. I think that's how Anna came by most of her interesting flavorings called for in so many of her recipes.

Rawleigh and Watkins salesmen traveled about in horse-drawn buggies during the 1910's, peddling their vast array of household products and baking aids to rural housewives who might not otherwise be able to purchase such products at their local grocery. Cookbooks often accompanied assortments of spices and flavoring extracts which included recipes for the use of their products and offered medical testimonials from satisfied customers for the tonics as well.

Flavors like Extract of White Rose and Jamaica Ginger aren't commonly used today, but they weren't unusual extracts in Anna's day. The one exception is Zephyr extract called for in recipe no. 122, Delicious Cookies on page 128. I've searched high and low for this product and it escapes me like a zephyr wind! It turns out that Zephyrus was the Greek God of the West Wind. A zephyr wind is sort of an elusive, refreshing, light breeze. Elusive is right! The culinary historians I asked about the product were stumped as well. It is therefore my obligation to make up ... err, I mean postulate, a theory about this odd flavoring.

I don't believe "Zephyr" was actually a flavor. I think it was the name of a company that sold elixirs, tonics, and flavorings as well. The recipe calls for colored icing, so I'd say that Delicious Cookies were part of the fancy, dainty dessert craze of the early 1900's. Most of the dainty desserts were flavored with either lemon or vanilla, so I'm guessing Zephyr extract is vanilla. That said, if anybody out there knows the truth about this flavoring, let me know and I'll send you a prize!

49. ANISE COOKIES

½ lb. butter, 4 teacups flour, 2 teacups sugar, 4 teaspoons baking powder, juice & rind of 1 lemon, ½ cup milk, 2 eggs, & flavor with anise. Roll out & cut fancy shape cookies. Brush over with egg & sprinkle over them sugar or when baked, or spread a coating made as follows. Mix powdered sugar with extract of lemon beaten with white of an egg.

Note: Use only 2 tsp. baking powder. Powdered egg white is recommended for the icing to avoid possible bacterial contamination from uncooked egg.

ICEBOX ANISE SEED COOKIES

1 cup butter	1 tsp. baking powder
1½ cup sugar	3 cups flour
2 eggs	¼ tsp. salt
2 tsp. whole anise seeds	Grated rind of a lemon

Cream butter and sugar; add eggs and beat well. Stir in lemon rind and anise seeds. Sift dry ingredients and add to creamed mixture. Chill the dough until firm and form into a log shape. Wrap in waxed paper and freeze until firm enough to slice about ¼ inch thick. Bake about 10 minutes at 400° until lightly browned.

INTERESTING FLAVORS

The next three anise-flavored cookies are a variation of Springerle, an ancient picture cookie of German origin. They are traditionally made using hartshorn (ammonium carbonate) as the leavening. The non-purist can substitute baking powder. Here's a typical Springerle recipe:

4½ cups flour	4 eggs
2 cups sugar	1 tsp. baking powder
Zest of a lemon (optional)	2 Tbs. anise seed

Beat the eggs until fluffy, gradually add sugar and beat at least 15 minutes with mixer. Sift baking powder and flour, then add to egg mixture. Refrigerate dough 2 hours, then roll out on floured board ½ inch thick. Press carved molds on dough or roll with springerle rolling pin. Cut cookies apart and let sit in cool room covered with a towel for 24 hrs. Drying the dough keeps the picture when baked. Grease a baking sheet and sprinkle with anise seeds. Moisten bottoms of cookies with a bit of water and place on baking sheet. Make a test cookie! Bake at 300° for 18 or so minutes. The cookies should be cooked but not brown.

95. SWISS COOKIES

Beat well the yelks of 5 eggs, 1 lb. sugar, sift in 1 lb. flour & 1 tablespoon anise seed. Beat all together well. Whip the whites of 5 eggs to a stiff froth, add, & beat all briskly. Roll out an inch thick & cut small size cookies. Set aside & bake next day. Heat the bake sheet & rub with bees wax. Let the tin cool again, wipe & lay on the cookies. Bake a light brown.

If you see the word yelk (as in egg yolk) in a receipt (recipe), it's at least of 19th century origin. Note that recipes 95 and 110 call the baker to "grease the pan with bees wax."

110. ANISE DROPS

3 cups sugar, & 6 eggs beaten together one half hour. Add 1 quart flour, ½ teaspoon extract essence of anise. Grease the pan with bees-wax & drop the mixture from spoon.

INTERESTING FLAVORS

168. ANISE SEED COOKIES

Beat 8 eggs & 1 lb. sugar together 30 minutes, then add 1 tablespoon anise seed, 1 lb. (scant) flour, 1 teaspoon baking powder, & roll out thin. Cut in fancy shapes bake in a quick oven.

Royal Baking Powder and Pastry Cook, 1911

104. SPENCER COOKIES

2 cups sugar, 8 eggs, 1½ pints flour, 1 teaspoon baking powder, 2 tablespoons coriander seed, 1 teaspoon extract lemon. Beat eggs & sugar together until they get thick & white. Add flour with powder, seed, extract, mix into a thick sponge. Drop in spoonfuls on greased pan. Bake in hot oven 5 or 6 minutes.

Royal Baking Powder & Pastry Cook, 1911

112. ALMOND JUMBLES COOKIES

1 lb. sugar, ½ lb. flour, ½ lb. butter, 1 teaspoon of sour milk, 5 eggs, 2 teaspoons extract of white rose, ¾ lb. of almonds (blanched and chopped fine), 1 teaspoon soda. Mix well, add whites of eggs beaten stiff last. Drop on buttered paper & bake quickly.

51. CARAWAY COOKIES

⅓ cup butter, 1 cup sugar, 1 egg, ⅔ cup milk, 4 cups flour, 2 heaping teaspoon baking powder, add 2 teaspoons caraway seed. Mix soft & drop on tin & bake.

203. TEA CAKES

3 cups flour, 1½ teaspoons baking powder, ½ teaspoon salt, ⅔ cup sugar, 3 tablespoons butter, 1 teaspoon caraway seed, milk to mix to soft biscuit dough. Roll out ¼ inch, cut in circles & bake in hot oven.

INTERESTING FLAVORS

164. DROP CARROT COOKIES

Mix 2 cups carrot marmalade, ½ cup melted butter, pinch salt, 2 eggs, 2 cups flour, 2 teaspoons baking powder, 1 teacup (scant) sugar, 3 or 4 tablespoons cream. Mix & beat well. Drop with teaspoon on greased tins & press or pat down so to spread with spoon.

TO COOK CARROT MARMALADE

Grate 2 big cups of carrots, add 1 cup sugar, 1 lemon, juice, grated rind, & pulp all. Mix well & let stand over night. In the morning boil in its own juice till very tender.

WONDERFUL! You have to make these delicious, healthy, beautiful cookies. See below for a couple of adjustments to the cookie recipe and more detailed instructions for preparing the marmalade.

Cream 10 Tbs. softened butter with the scant cup sugar, then blend in 2 eggs and add 1 tsp. vanilla. Sift 1 tsp. baking powder and ½ tsp. salt, with 2 cups of flour and add to the above mixture. Omit the cream. Blend in marmalade and drop by spoonfuls onto parchment paper. Bake at 350° until lightly browned.

To make marmalade:

Grate about 6 organic, peeled carrots to equal 2 cups. (Organic carrots will taste better and are a brighter orange.) Carefully peel the yellow rind from a lemon, avoiding the bitter white part. Chop rind well. Combine carrots, 1 cup sugar, the rind and juice of the lemon, and refrigerate overnight. Next day, simmer mixture on lowest heat until just about all the liquid is absorbed and the carrots are translucent and "candied." It will take about 30 minutes, and needs to be watched carefully at the end so the mixture doesn't burn. Cool, then add to cookie batter above.

Other Uses for Carrot Marmalade

Add to your favorite pound cake recipe before baking, make carrot marmalade pinwheel cookies, add to oatmeal cookie batter, put on your morning toast, add a dab to steamed carrots, soften with a little rum and spread between layers of carrot cake.

INTERESTING FLAVORS

Reading Tea Leaves, 1892

193. COFFEE COOKIES

2 cups brown sugar, 1 cup shortning, 2 eggs, 1 cup cold
strong coffee, 1 teaspoon soda dissolved in water, 1 cup
raisins, 1 teaspoon nutmeg, 2 teaspoons baking powder, & 3 cups flour. Drop from spoon in pan & bake, or
use flour enough to roll, then cut and bake.

This cookie is OK as written, but I'd use half a cup of coffee instead of
a whole cup. Even still, the coffee flavor will be very faint, so add a
teaspoon of instant coffee for a more intense flavor. Cardamom marries well with coffee, if you're not a nutmeg fan.

Company
Home Secrets, 1898

•*To accidentally place a teakettle on the stove with the spout
toward the back, is a sign of company.*
•*If paper burns on top of the stove, it is a sign of company.*
•*If the coffee pot rocks on the stove, it is a sign of a visitor.*

122. DELICIOUS COOKIES

1 cup sugar, ½ cup butter, 2 eggs, ½ cup milk, 1½ cups flour, 1 teaspoon baking powder. Flavor with extract of zephyr. Bake in small crescent shaped tins. Make a boiled frosting & color with any fruit colors. These are dainty served with afternoon teas. By making this batter stiff, you may drop cookies in baking sheet & bake instead of small crescent tins.

Photo courtesy Library of Congress

Traveling silverware salesman, 1940

184. RHUBARB COOKIES

1 cup rhubarb, 1 cup shortning, 1 cup sugar, pinch salt, 1 teaspoon cinnamon, ½ teaspoon cloves, dash of nutmeg, ½ teaspoon soda dissolved in rhubarb, 2 cups flour, 2 teaspoons baking powder, 1 cup each of chopped raisins, currants, & nut meats. Mix & drop in greased pans. Bake.

NOVELTY

CIGARETTES COOKIES

Anna found many of her recipes in Royal Baking Powder Cook Books, but here's one from 1902 that she somehow overlooked. The Royal recipes were usually pretty good, but this clovey cookie sounds too horrible to even try. I can see why Anna passed it up.

Mix and sift 2 cups flour, 1 teaspoon Royal Baking Powder, 2 tablespoons sugar, ½ teaspoon salt. Rub in 2 tablespoons butter, add ½ teaspoon extract cinnamon, 10 drops extract cloves, and milk to mix to a rather firm dough. Knead till smooth, cut off bits size of hickory nuts and mold into shapes of cigarettes. Take ½ cup granulated sugar and 1 teaspoon powdered cinnamon, mix, and roll each cigarette in it. Lay on greased pans, bake in moderate oven.

27. CASTOR OIL COOKIES

1 cup each of sugar, molasses, & milk, ½ cup castor oil, pinch of salt, 1 teaspoon soda, 2 teaspoons ginger, & enough flour to make a dough that can be rolled. Roll out, cut in shapes & bake in quick oven. Two of these cookies are equal to a dose of castor oil, & children eat them readily.

Courtesy of University of Louisville

WARNING: Not that anybody on the entire planet would consider making castor oil cookies in this day and time, I have to add a caution, just in case. Castor Oil is a stimulant laxative. Follow package directions for appropriate dosage. More than a couple of these cookies will wreak havoc on your innards and could be harmful. Even though moms have been castor oiling up their kids for generations to keep things "moving along," don't give these to children. Better yet, don't give these to anybody!

WORLD WAR I COOKIES

America reluctantly entered World War I on April 6, 1917. One month later, the Food Administration, headed by Herbert Hoover, would be formed in order to provide food for our troops at war, our allies abroad, and those at home. American housewives were asked to conserve white flour, butter, sugar, and eggs so that these goods could be exported as well as stored for inevitable postwar food shortages worldwide.

Bad news for Anna, the cookie queen, but she rose to the occasion with both work boots on. She and other early 20th-century housewives weren't strangers to ingredient shortages anyway. Outdoor chickens didn't do much egg laying in the winter months where Anna lived, so I'm sure it wasn't that much of a stretch to reach for favored eggless cookie recipes. And don't you know the baking powder industry was happy to lend a hand by reminding mothers that their product was a dandy replacement for eggs in baked goods.

Substituting cornmeal, buckwheat, rye, barley, and oats for white flour had to have been a whole different matter. You might first look at these recipes and say, "Blah! Who would eat THAT?" I say these

recipes were a testimony to the resilience of the American spirit, everyone doing their part. Besides, these whole grain, low fat, not too sweet cookies really are good for you, and with a little tweaking they can even be a creative alternative for the wheat intolerant.

American food conservation efforts continued for two years from May 1917 until June 1919, basically covering most of the time when Anna was recording her cookie recipes. Many of the recipes in other chapters of this book reflect ingredient shortages, but those that you will find in this chapter are dramatic examples of patriotic make-do baking.

101. RICE COOKIES

½ cup butter, 1½ cups sugar, 4 eggs, 1½ cup rice flour, 1 teaspoon baking powder, ½ cup cream, 1 teaspoon extract lemon. Beat the eggs & sugar together 10 minutes; add the butter (melted). Sift together flour, rice flour, & powder, and add to the eggs mixture. Mix in thin batter & bake in patty pans, or mix rather a stiff batter & drop by spoon well apart & bake in hot oven.

Photo by Wes Erbsen

Now here's a lovely, crispy cookie with a rich buttery lemon flavor....and the chalky mouth-feel of a chewable antacid. But as we've learned to say around here: "They're better than no cookie." The tasters actually loved them. Anna didn't specify how much flour to add, so I made them like this:

¼ cup butter	¾ cup rice flour
¾ cup sugar	½ tsp. baking powder
1 egg	¼ tsp. salt
½ tsp. lemon extract*	¼ cup all purpose flour
3 tablespoons whipping cream	

Cream butter and sugar, add egg and blend. Stir in lemon flavoring, then when combined add a few tablespoons whipping cream. Stir salt and baking powder into the rice flour and blend with wet ingredients. Add about ¼ cup flour, or maybe a tad more, and drop dough into a log form on waxed paper. Roll up and freeze until firm. Slice about ⅓ inch thick, decorate, and bake about 11 minutes at 375°. I'm not big on eggy cookies, so I didn't try beating the four eggs and sugar for 10 minutes. That would probably make for a puffier cookie, maybe with a better texture. Anna left the plain flour out of her ingredient list in her recipe, but mentioned it later on in the instructions, so I suspect she would have added about ½ cup to her original recipe.

*Note: You can substitute half a grated lemon rind for the lemon flavoring if you prefer the taste of fresh lemon. Reverse amounts of all purpose and rice flour for a less chalky texture.

WORLD WAR I COOKIES

she is doing her part to help win the war

Courtesy Library of Congress

World War I Cookies

121. Fancy Cookies

2 cups brown sugar, ½ cup lard, 2 eggs, 4 tablespoons warm water, ½ cup butter, ½ cup sour cream, ½ teaspoon soda, pinch salt & little nutmeg. 1 cup of shelled pumpkin seeds improves them.

Note: Anna omitted the flour, so I'm guessing you add enough to make a stiff dough that you can roll and cut with cookie cutters.

176. Rolled Oat Crisps Cookies

Beat 2 eggs, add ¾ cup brown sugar, beat well again. Add ½ teaspoon salt, ½ teaspoon vanilla, 1 tablespoon melted shortning, 2½ cups rolled oats. Mix well & drop small piles well apart on greased pan. Bake in quick oven until crisp & brown.

This recipe was all over the place in the first two decades of the 20th century. I found it in no less than 10 cookbooks from that era. Cynthia Van Deusen, friend and fellow cookie enthusiast, courageously offered to test the recipe. She loved the granola-like texture of the cookie that's crunchy on the outside and a bit chewy in the middle.

Being fascinated by their enduring popularity, I figured I had to make them myself as well to see what all the fuss was about. I halved the recipe and added a little extra butter and brown sugar. Then, I thought I'd just toast the oats first to ensure a crunchy cookie. Sure enough, the little piles of brown sugar glazed toasted oats held together by just enough egg mixture were just great...but I couldn't stop there. Somehow it seemed like toasted walnuts would be a nice addition, and toasted coconut, and wheat germ toasted with a little butter and maple syrup, and after adding toasted sesame seeds, I stopped. I stopped only because I was eyeing the chocolate chips and the dried cherries, apricots, and raisins and you just can't toast them.

The consensus from tasters is that both versions are excellent. If you add other toasted ingredients, be sure to reduce the oats proportionally.

If your apron becomes untied it is an indication that somebody is speaking of you.   *Home Secrets,* 1898

WORLD WAR I COOKIES

185. RHUBARB MARMALADE SAND DROPS

1 cup rhubarb marmalade, 1 cup melted shortening, 3 tablespoons sugar, pinch salt, 1 teaspoon cinnamon, ½ scant cloves, ¼ teaspoon nutmeg, ½ teaspoon soda dissolved in rhubarb marmalade, 1 cup pumpkin seed or squash seed shelled, ½ cup corn meal (yellow), ½ cup wheat flour, 2 teaspoons baking powder. Mix & beat well & bake in moderate oven 8 or 10 minutes.

RHUBARB MARMALADE, SCOTCH RECIPE

"Give us a vote and we will cook."

Just in case you need some rhubarb marmalade, here's a recipe I found in a fun book that was published in 1908, called *The Washington Women's Cook Book* by The Washington Equal Suffrage Association. The dedication of the book reads:

> *"To the first woman who realized that half the human race were not getting a square deal and who had the courage to voice a protest; and also to the long line of women from that day unto this who saw clearly though strongly and braved misrepresentation, ridicule, calumny, and social ostracism to bring about that millennial day when humanity shall know the blessedness of dwelling together as equals."*

"Cut rhubarb fine and put pound of sugar to pound of fruit; let stand for two nights then pour off syrup and cook until it thickens, then add the rhubarb and figs, one pound of figs to seven pounds of rhubarb. Add green ginger if desired."

Try this: Use 2 cups chopped rhubarb and one heaping cup sugar. Let sit overnight, pour off syrup, adding about ¼ cup water and boil off half the liquid on low heat. Be careful not to let the mixture burn. Add rhubarb and cook until thick. Cool, then use the marmalade in the above cookie recipe if you're brave, or add to your favorite sugar cookie recipe. Decrease sugar in the recipe to compensate for the sweetened rhubarb and add chopped walnuts and raisins if you like. I prefer to use the rhubarb marmalade as the filling for thumbprint sugar cookies. The flavor tends to get lost, believe it or not, in the sugar cookie dough, but it sure makes for a pretty cookie.

WORLD WAR I COOKIES

Ladies Ladling Preserves

Courtesy Library of Congress

WORLD WAR I COOKIES

OATMEAL MACAROONS
Royal Baking Powder Cookbook, 1918

1 egg
½ cup sugar
1 tablespoon shortening
½ teaspoon salt

2 teaspoons Royal Baking Powder
2 cups rolled oats
1 teaspoon vanilla
¼ cup corn syrup

Beat egg yolk and white separately. Cream sugar with melted shortening. Add egg yolk, syrup, salt and oatmeal. Then add baking powder, white of egg and vanilla. Mix thoroughly, drop on greased pan about half teaspoon to each macaroon. Allow space for spreading. Bake about 10 minutes in moderate oven. Cool before removing from pan.

Royal Baking Powder Co., 1918

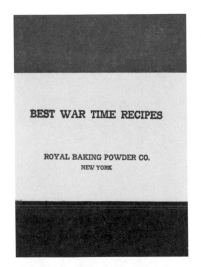

BEST WAR TIME RECIPES

ROYAL BAKING POWDER CO.
NEW YORK

" This booklet is dedicated to the housewives of the United States who are assisting the Government in its work through the Food Administration. The recipes have been carefully tested and if used according to directions will make delicious, wholesome and appetizing food.

The different kinds of flour specified in the recipes have been recommended by the U. S. Food Administration to be used in place of white flour. If any of them are not readily obtainable, other non-wheat flours which are available may often be substituted with good results."

World War I Cookies

177. Nut Crisps Cookie

1 tablespoon butter, 1 cup sugar, 2 eggs, pinch salt, 2 ½ cups rolled oats (or a little more), 2 level teaspoons baking powder. Drop by teaspoon on well buttered pan & bake in slow oven. Shelled pumpkin or squash seeds are equal to blanched almonds for cookies or cakes.

There are no nuts in this recipe! From the above reference to pumpkin or squash seeds, I'd guess ½ to 1 cup of blanched almonds were called for in original recipe.

178. & 183. War Cookies

Into your mixing bowl put:
2 cups rolled oats, ½ cup warm water, ¾ cup molasses, 2 tablespoons cooking oil (or melted shortning), 1 teaspoon each of salt, sinnamon, ½ teaspoon of ginger, cloves, & soda. Mix well & add 2 cups of graham flour, with which dredge ½ cup each of chopped peanuts & small raisins. Drop by teaspoon on greased tins & bake about 20 minutes. Press a large flattened raisin on top of each cookie while hot.

Photo courtesy Library of Congress

Mrs. Calvin Coolidge munches a girl scout cookie, 1923

WORLD WAR I COOKIES

179. HONEY COOKIES

1 cupful honey, 1 cup sour cream, 1 egg, 1 teaspoon (scant) of soda, 1 teaspoon salt, 1 heaping teaspoon cinnamon, flour enough to roll out. These are better the second day.

181. MASHED POTATO COOKIES

1½ cups mashed potatoes, 1 cup sugar, 1 cup fat, 1¾ cups wheat flour, 2 teaspoons baking powder, 1 teaspoon cinnamon, ½ teaspoon cloves, ½ teaspoon nutmeg. Nuts & raisins may be added. Mix in the order given & drop onto a greased pan and bake in a moderate oven about 20 minutes. Saves 40% wheat flour.

Now how can you possibly resist trying this cookie? I made these just as written, using butter for the fat, and whole wheat flour. Since Anna referred to whole wheat flour as graham flour, and alternative flours like rye and barley were being used in baking during the war, it's possible this recipe called for white flour. But it's the ultimate make-do cookie, so I made a whole grain version. As I sheepishly handed a plate of them to my husband, Wayne, I posed the question: "Would you rather have this cookie or no cookie?" After eating four of them, he said, "Why wouldn't I want to eat this cookie?" So, there you have it. For a truly tasty alternative, substitute sweet potato, brown sugar, butter, and white flour for like ingredients. Use plenty of spices, nuts, and raisins.

WORLD WAR I COOKIES

Lydia Pinkham's War-Time Cook and Health Book
July, 1917

Printed at the request of the department of food conservation July 23, 1917.

SOMETHING FOR MAMMA.

Manufactured by the
HECKER JONES JEWELL MILLING CO.
NEW YORK.

Save Wheat
Order bread twenty-four hours in advance so your baker will not bake beyond his needs. Cut the loaf on the table and only as required. Use stale bread for cooking, toast, etc. Eat less cake and pastry.

Use All The Milk
The children must have whole milk. Therefore use less cream. Use every drop of skim milk. Use buttermilk and sour milk for cooking and cottage cheese.

Save The Fats
We are the world's greatest fat wasters. Fat is food. Use butter on the table as usual, but not in cooking. Other fats are as good in cooking. Reduce fried foods. Save daily one-third ounce animal fats. Soap contains fats. Do not waste it. Make homemade soap.

Save The Sugar
Our Allies need sugar, and sugar is getting scarcer. We use today three times as much per person as our Allies. So there may be enough for all at a reasonable price, use less candy and sweet drinks. Do not skimp in putting up fruit and jams, to use in place of butter.

Use More Fruits And Vegetables
We have them in abundance. As a nation we eat too little green stuffs. Double their use and improve your health.

Use Local Supplies
Patronize your home producer. Distance means money. Buy perishable food from the region nearest you and thus save transportation.

182. SHORTS COOKIES PLAIN
1 cup shortning, 2 cups sugar, ¾ cup sweet milk, 2 eggs, 2 cups shorts, 3 cups flour, 3 teaspoons baking powder. Roll thin & bake quickly. Flavor to taste.

Having never heard of an ingredient called "shorts," and knowing full well that early 20th century fashion dictated that legs be covered by clothing, I assumed folks wouldn't be hanging around wearing short pants munching on cookies. So, then I figured that "shorts" must be wheat germ since the germ of a wheat plant contains oil, or shortening, which would also save on white flour when used for baking during WWI. So I doctored up Anna's recipe just a bit and created a killer cookie quite by accident.

Help Win the War

Woman's Service Requires Health & Strength

War-Time

Cook and Health Book

Then my research led me to the real explanation of "shorts." When wheat is milled, there are three coproducts that are separated out during the process. The bran is a coarse product while the finer bran-like substance is called "shorts," and then there is the germ. While bran cookies are good for you, so are these vitamin and mineral-packed strikingly crunchy and nutty wheat-germ flavored jewels. (See facing page.)

WORLD WAR I COOKIES

YUMMY TOASTED WHEAT GERM COOKIES

½ cup butter	1 cup flour
½ cup brown sugar	1 tsp. baking powder
½ cup white sugar	½ tsp. salt
1 egg	1 cup wheat germ, plain
1 tsp. vanilla	3 Tbs. maple syrup
½ cup currants (optional)	1 Tbs. butter

Melt the 1 Tbs. butter in a pie plate and stir in the maple syrup. Add germ and mix well until well coated. Toast in 350° oven for about 10 minutes until light brown. Cool. (Stick the hot wheat germ on a bit of foil and chill it in the freezer if you're in a hurry.) Cream butter and sugars. If you prefer a less sweet cookie, cut the white sugar in half. Add egg and blend, stir in vanilla. Sift together flour, baking powder and salt, and add to creamed mixture. When germ is totally cool, stir that in along with the currants. Drop on greased baking sheet or parchment and bake at 375° about 10 minutes until lightly browned.

PRESERVE PERISHABLE PRODUCE

HOME CANNER

IF YOU HAVE A FRUIT GARDEN YOU OUGHT TO USE A CANNER

Food Production Dept., 72, Victoria St. London, S.W.

Dampened clothes will not mildew for several days if you put them into the lower part of the refrigerator.

Dr. Sloan's Hints to Housekeepers, 1920

191. WAR COOKIES

1½ cup molasses, ½ cup cooking oil or lard, 1 cup left-over coffee (from meal), 1 teaspoon each of soda, cinnamon, ginger, & pinch salt & flour to mix stiff. Mix over night & keep in cool place till morning, when you will be able to roll out the dough. Take a portion at a time, without the addition of much more flour. Bake in a quick oven.

202. RYE DROP CAKES

1 heaping cup rye meal, 1 heaping cup flour, pinch salt, 3 tablespoons molasses, 1 cup milk, 2 eggs, 2⅓ teaspoons baking powder. Sift dry materials together. Add milk, molasses, & beaten eggs. Drop by spoonfuls.

209. BARLEY & ROLLED OAT DROP COOKIES

Cream together: 1 cup fat, ¼ cup brown sugar, add ½ cup corn syrup, 1 egg, beaten. Mix 1 cup barley flour, 2 teaspoons baking powder, pinch salt, ½ teaspoon cinnamon. Add to the first & mix well & then add ½ cup nutmeats & 1 cup raisins. Drop from teaspoon on well greased tins & bake in moderate oven.

U.S. Agriculture in Comfort

JUGG... THE Land-Agent

213. HONEY COOKIES

Beat 1 egg, add ¼ cup honey slowly & 1 tablespoon melted fat. Mix & sift ½ cup rye flour, ¼ cup white flour, ¾ teaspoon baking powder, ¼ teaspoon salt, then add ¼ cup chopped of each raisins & nutmeats. Drop from spoon on well greased tins & bake in a moderate oven for about 20 minutes. *Lady's Home Journal*

WORLD WAR I COOKIES

The Faithful Hen
by C. E. Miller, *Farm & Home*, Feb. 1918

The gentle hen, black, red, or white,
 I love with all my heart.
She gives me eggs with all her might,
 To eat or take to mart.

She never loafs, or sulks, or strikes,
 She's up at early morn.
She thanks me with her song, she likes,
 Her wheat and oats and corn.

She wanders scratching here and there
 To find a bug or seed;
And be the weather foul or fair,
 Her song's still heard, indeed.

And when, at last, her race is run,
 And her last egg we've got,
We still enjoy her, if well done,
 In roaster, pan, or pot.

SECRETS FROM THE KITCHEN

The maiden that is unfortunate enough to upset a tub of water, must prepare for trouble; if she marries, her husband will be poor, lazy, and a spendthrift.

When bread, cake or pie will burn in spite of you, your husband or lover is angry.

When soup continues to boil after the kettle has been taken off, the cook will live to a good old age.

To forget to put coffee in the coffee pot is a sure sign of a prize.

If a cork pops out of a bottle suddenly, you have an unknown enemy.

If you sing while making bread, you will cry before it is eaten.

If your apron becomes untied it is an indication that somebody is speaking of you.

If a young girl spills water while putting it into any vessel, or while carrying it, it is a sign her lover is drinking to her health.

Home Secrets, 1898

WOMEN AND COOKIES

You'd think we women could figure out our role as cookie bakers in the home vs. employees in the workplace by now. After all, the debate didn't start with the wife of a 1992 American presidential candidate when she said, "I could have stayed home and baked cookies and had tea parties instead of having a career." You need look no further than the turn-of-the-20th-century women's suffrage movement to see that we've been working this one out for a long, long time in this country.

Anna gives us no indication in her cookie diary of where she stood on the issue of women's rights. Few middle-class urban women were college educated or worked outside the home at the time that she recorded her cookie recipes.  But that didn't keep them from turning out in large numbers to fight for the right to vote. Sandwiched between the Victorian era, when maids did much of the family cooking, and 1920 when modern appliances saved housewives time enough to do for themselves, we'll never know what Anna was thinking on the subject of women's suffrage. As she stood at the board rolling out dough, did she say to herself, *"Why am I at home baking cookies when I could be out marching for the vote?"* Or, maybe, *"I've got to get all these cookies made for the women-vote meeting tonight."* Then again, she could have said to herself, *"There's nothing I love more than staying home and caring for my house and family to the aroma of fresh baked gingersnaps."*

I'm just glad that after being dragged into the fray, the art of cookie-baking is still alive and well in America. No matter what side of the cookie fence you stand on, let's be sure to keep those torpedo shaped refrigerated rolls of slice-off dough on the grocery store shelves where they belong, and take the time to bake the real thing. A hundred years from now, when we're still debating where women ought to be, I hope we're hashing it out over a plate of warm Snickerdoodles.

WOMEN AND COOKIES

Courtesy of the Library of Congress

1909 Women's Suffrage Poster

Anna's Manuscript

Plain molasses Cookies

Mix: 1 cup molasses, ½ cup lard [melted], ½ cup [scant] of sour milk, pinch salt, 1 teaspoon soda, & flour enough to rollout in a sheet not too thick. cut & bake in moderate oven. 1 heaping teaspoon ginger may be added.

Graham cookies

mix
2 cups sugar, ½ cup lard [melted] 2 eggs, – ad. 2 cups sour milk, 2 level teaspoons soda, 2 cups graham flour, 1 cup white flour, & mix as for cookies. Roll out thin, – cut & bake in moderate oven.

Fancy cookies

Mix: 2 cups brown sugar, 1 cup shortning, 2 eggs, ½ cup sour cream or [milk] pinch salt, ½ teaspoon [scant] of nutmeg, & 4 table spoons of warm water in which dissolve ½ teaspoon soda. Flour enough to roll out. You can make different shape cookies out of this dough, Wash some with milk, & sprinkle with [colored course sugar] others sprinkle with currants, & some with cocoanut.   Bake in slow oven.

Rock cookies

Mix well 1 ½ cups brown sugar, 1 cup butter, or (lard) pinch salt, 1 teaspoon cinnamon, 2 eggs, 3 table spoons sour cream (milk or butter milk) with 1 teaspoon soda,. Ad. 2 cups flour, ½ cup raisins, ½ cup currants, [sprinkled with flour], mix all well together; roll out & cut. mark each cookie crosswise with a fork & bake.

THANKS!

Thanks to Steve Millard for cover design. Proof readers included Jessica Boing, David Currier, Richard Renfro, and Janet Swell. Thanks to Jennifer Drake Thomas for recipe editing, and to cookie photographers Wes Erbsen and Leon Swell. Recipe testers included Cynthia Van Deusen, Marti Otto, and Richard Refro. Thanks also to culinary historians Linda Stradley (www.whatscookingamerica.net) and Lynne Olver (www.thefoodtimeline.org) for their expertise.

There were no shortage of cookie tasters for this project, but the cookie monster prize goes to David Currier, our marketing director, who never met a cookie he didn't love. Our shipper, Kelli Churchill, happily met the relentless demands of cookie tasting as well. Other tasters included my kids, Annie, Wes, and Rita Erbsen (along with all of their friends who walked into the house this year), Sara and Courtney Webb, Sam Sematus, Janet Swell, Roger, Jessie, and Ezra Burns, Nancy and Leon Swell, Laura, David, Abbie, Liz, and Colin Wright, Randy Greenberg, Capper Tramm, Effie Price, Jennifer, Neil, and Cece Thomas, Jonah, Paul, and Wyndy Bonesteel, Evan, Carson, and Bryce Van Deusen, Marti Otto, Richard, Maya, and Zoe Renfro, and Rob and Wanda Levin. (Wanda was the winner of the 1965 Betty Crocker *Homemaker of Tomorrow* award. If she can't taste-test a cookie, now who could?) More tasting thanks goes to Ms. Donalyn's 4th grade class at Isaac Dickson Elementary in Asheville, NC, most of the 5th graders at Haw Creek Elementary in Asheville, and Slow Food Asheville.

Finally, thanks to my husband/publisher, Wayne Erbsen, who has officially been busted by the cookie police for his overzealous cookie-gobbling behavior. I'm going to have to write a dainty salad green cookbook next so we can all get back into shape!

BIBLIOGRAPHY

COOKBOOKS

All Saints Episcopal Church, *Recipes From Pawley's Island*, 1955
Author Unknown, *The Cook Not Mad*, 1831
Author Unknown, The Cookie Jar, 1950's fund-raising cookbook
Author Unknown, *Quick Cooking,* 1880's
Bailey, Pearl, *Domestic Science Principles & Application*, 1924
Farmer, Fannie Merritt, *Boston Cooking School Cook Book*, 1896-1918
Friends of the Church of the Brethren, *Inglenook Cook Book,* 1911
Gillette, F.L., & Ziemann, Hugo, *The White House Cook Book*, 1887
Ladies' Aid Society of the First Presbyterian Church, Marion, Ohio,
      Recipes Tried and True, 1894
Ladies Club of Illinois, *The New Home Cook Book*, 1925
Larkin Co., *Larkin Housewives Cook Book*, 1915
Morris, Josephine, *Household Science and Arts*, 1915
Parloa, Maria, *Miss Parloa's New Cook Book*, 1882
Randolph, Mary, *The Virginia House-wife*, 1824
Simmons, Amelia, *American Cookery,* Facsimile, 1796
Thomas, Edith M., *Mary At The Farm and Book of Recipes Compiled
      During Her Visit Among The Pennsylvania Germans*, 1915
Wales Ladies Aid, *Favorite Cookie Recipes*, probably 1940's
Ward, Artemas. *The Grocer's Encyclopedia*, 1911
Washington Equal Suffrage Association, *The Washington Women's
      Cook Book,* compiled by Linda Deziah Jennings, 1908
Wells, Robert, *Bread & Biscuit Bakers & Sugar Boiler's Assistant, 1890*
White, Mrs. Peter A, *The Kentucky Cookery Book*, 1885

POPULAR MAGAZINES

Comfort Magazine, May, 1910
Farm and Fireside, May 1910
Farm and Home, Feb. 1918
Ladies World, June 1897, Feb., 1898
Rural New Yorker, July, 1926
The Farmer's Wife, Dec., 1909
The Modern Priscilla, Oct., 1909, Sept., 1912, Jan., June, Sept., Oct.,
1915, Jan., 1917
The People's Home Journal, January-June, 1907
Woman's World, May 1913
Sears & Roebuck Catalogue, 1896

BIBLIOGRAPHY

ADVERTISING COOKBOOKS

Choice Recipes, Walter Baker & Co., 1916

Cow Brand Soda Cook Book and Facts Worth Knowing, 1918

Davis Baking Powder Recipes, 1922

Dr. Miles Nervine Cook Book, 1920

Dr. Ward's Medical Company Cook Book, (wagon delivered remedies, flavorings, spices, and household supplies), no date, about 1910

Food and Health, Lydia Pinkham's Vegetable Compound, 1915

Home Comfort Cook Book, 1933

Home Secrets, Pabst Blue Ribbon Company, 1898

How to Save Eggs by Using Dr. Price's Cream Baking Powder, 1917

Iced Dainties, Oklahoma Ice Manufacturers Association, 1928

Majestic Range Cook Book, 1911

Matilda's Proven Sparton Recipes, Sparton Refrigerators, about 1928

Mrs. Winslow's Domestic Receipt Book, 1872

Practical Handbook on Leavening, The Rumford Company, 1936

The Quality Cook Book, Roberts & Mander Stove Co., 1930

Reliable Recipes, Calumet Baking Powder, 1920

Royal Baking Powder Cook Book, 1902, 1911, 1920

Rumford Baking Powder Common Sense Cook Book, 1920

Sloan's Handy Hints & Up-to-Date Cook Book, 1901

Snowdrift Secrets, Sarah Tyson Rorer, Southern Cotton Oil Co., 1913

Tummy Tingles, Wheat Flour Institute, 1937

War Time Cook & Health Book, Lydia Pinkham, 1917

HANDWRITTEN COOKING MANUSCRIPTS

In addition to Anna's cookie diary, approximately 25 antique hand-written cooking manuscripts from the author's personal collection were consulted for this project. The journals ranged in date from the 1840's through the 1950's.

RECIPE INDEX

RECIPE INDEX

NATIVE GROUND MUSIC

BOOKS OF SONGS & LORE
Backpocket Bluegrass Songbook
Backpocket Old-Time Songbook
Cowboy Songs, Jokes & Lingo
Front Porch Songs & Stories
Old-Time Gospel Songbook
Outlaw Ballads, Legends, & Lore
Railroad Fever
Rousing Songs of the Civil War
Log Cabin Pioneers
Rural Roots of Bluegrass

INSTRUCTION BOOKS
5-String Banjo for the
      Complete Ignoramus!
Bluegrass Banjo Simplified!!
Painless Guide to the Guitar
Painless Mandolin Melodies
Southern Mountain Banjo
Southern Mountain Fiddle
Southern Mountain Guitar
Southern Mountain Mandolin
Southern Mountain Dulcimer

RECORDINGS

Authentic Outlaw Ballads
Ballads & Songs of the Civil War
Bullfrogs on Your Mind
Cowboy Songs
Front Porch Favorites
Love Songs of the Civil War
The Home Front
Log Cabin Songs

Old-Time Gospel Favorites
Raccoon and a Possum
Railroadin' Classics
Railroad Fever
Singing Rails
Songs of the Santa Fe Trail
Southern Mountain Classics
Southern Soldier Boy

MORE HISTORIC COOKBOOKS BY BARBARA SWELL

Log Cabin Cooking
Take Two and Butter 'Em While They're Hot!
Children at the Hearth
Secrets of the Great Old-Timey Cooks
Mama's in the Kitchen
Old-Time Farmhouse Cooking
The Lost Art of Pie Making Made Easy

Write or call for a FREE Catalog:
Native Ground Books & Music
109 Bell Road
Asheville, NC 28805
(800) 752-2656
www.nativeground.com   banjo@nativeground.com